THE POCKET BOOK OF
OLD MASTERS

Front cover illustration:
Beatrice d'Este by LEONARDO DA VINCI

Back cover illustration:
Young Woman with a Water Jug by VERMEER

THE POCKET BOOK OF OLD MASTERS

EDITED BY HERMAN J. WECHSLER

CONTAINING 64 REPRODUCTIONS OF PAINTINGS

BY DA VINCI, MICHELANGELO, REMBRANDT, RAPHAEL, TITIAN, BRUEGEL, VELASQUEZ, EL GRECO, RUBENS AND VERMEER

TEXT BY W. SOMERSET MAUGHAM, WALTER PATER, THOMAS CRAVEN, VIRGIL BARKER, HENDRIK WILLEM VAN LOON, ELIE FAURE, COUNT DE GOBINEAU, HIPPOLYTE TAINE, PHILIP HALE AND GIORGIO VASARI

POCKET BOOKS, INC., NEW YORK

POCKET BOOK EDITION PUBLISHED MARCH, 1949
1st printing............................February, 1949

THE TEXT OF THIS POCKET BOOK IS PRINTED
FROM BRAND-NEW PLATES MADE FROM NEWLY SET,
LARGE, CLEAR, EASY-TO-READ TYPE. THE ILLUS-
TRATIONS ARE PRINTED FROM NEW ENGRAVED
CYLINDERS MADE SPECIALLY FOR THIS EDITION.

ACKNOWLEDGMENTS

The editor wishes to acknowledge his indebtedness to the following publishers for permission to reprint from their original editions as indicated:

SIMON AND SCHUSTER, New York, for the Raphael selection from *Vasari's Lives of the Artists*, Copyright 1946 by Betty Burroughs,

HARPER AND BROTHERS, New York, for the Titian selection from *Renaissance Art* by Elie Faure, Copyright 1923 by Harper and Brothers,

THE ARTS, Gaylordsville, Conn., for the Pieter Bruegel selection from the September 1926 edition of that magazine, Copyright 1926 by *The Arts*,

LIVERIGHT PUBLISHING COMPANY, New York, for the Rembrandt selection from *R.V.R.* by Hendrik van Loon, Copyright 1930 by Horace Liveright,

DOUBLEDAY AND COMPANY, New York, for the El Greco selection from *Of Human Bondage* by Somerset Maugham, Copyright 1915 by George H. Doran Company,

SIMON AND SCHUSTER, New York, for the Velasquez selection from *Men of Art* by Thomas Craven, Copyright 1931 by Thomas Craven,

CHARLES T. BRANFORD COMPANY, Boston, for the Vermeer selection from *Vermeer* by Philip L. Hale, Copyright 1937 by Hale, Cushman and Flint, Incorporated.

CONTENTS

EDITOR'S INTRODUCTION

THE PURPOSE of this book is to show that Art
is really for Everyman, and that the language
of art criticism may be as simple and direct as the
statements of the artists themselves. We will
ignore the mysterious terms and phrases of that
"critic" who seems to think that his function is
to confuse rather than to clarify, who seems to
believe that simple declarative sentences are ta-
boo, and that his stature as a writer on art will
depend on the length and complexity of his para-
graphs. We hope to demonstrate to our readers
that there are men who have not been fearful of
introducing Heart and Sentiment into their
prose, men who write with passion, emotion and
imagination about the artists they admire. We
would like to think that the excerpts printed in
the following pages will cause many a reader to
seek further, to search for other writings of our
critics and other pictures by the artists here rep-
resented.

For our painters we have taken ten great figures out of the pageant of art history. With our

selection no man may quibble—the masters are all surely *great*. We, too, wish there were space for more of them: for Holbein, and Dürer, and Frans Hals, to name a few. But here none the less is a grand suite of names—Leonardo da Vinci, Michelangelo, Raphael, Titian, Bruegel, Rubens, Rembrandt, El Greco, Velasquez and Vermeer.

For the critics, our task was a more difficult one. Here we were tempted to prove our point: that the poet, the dramatist, the essayist, the novelist, as well as the historian, all may write aptly of Art and Artists. There surely is no single style or formula, as there certainly is no single style or manner for the painter himself. As the artist may cover a huge ceiling with frescoes, or a simple small wood panel or canvas to express himself, so may the writer employ a volume, an essay or a sonnet to convey to us his message. Therefore, we have selected passages from a novel by Somerset Maugham for the finest tribute to El Greco that we know. We have chosen a chapter from Hendrik Willem van Loon's *Life and Times of Rembrandt van Rijn* for an astonishing "imaginary conversation" between the artist and his biographer. We tried to indicate the variety of styles available by selecting Vasari's account of Raphael. Vasari's *Lives* has been used by almost every writer on the history of the Renaissance, from the sixteenth century to the present day. Arthur, Count de Gobineau, gives us a brilliantly

conceived dramatic sketch set in the studio of
Michelangelo. We quote from the scintillating
lecture notes of the French scholar Taine, as well
as from the two most widely read books on art
history of our own time, Elie Faure's *History of
Art* and *Men of Art* by Thomas Craven. We purposely include two scholarly essays, to show what
good art criticism is like, by Virgil Barker and
Philip Hale. In their respective pieces on Bruegel
and Vermeer, they demonstrate that writing on
art can be lucid, straightforward, and easy of
comprehension.

Centuries ago, people were less easily fright-
ened away from an informal and natural contact
with art. It was more a part of their daily life
and was accepted quite casually. The individual
encountered it when he went to church, when he
passed through the streets of his city, when he
entered a public building to have a paper signed
or stamped. Today, we seem to forget that the
painter or sculptor was once classed as a crafts-
man, a member of a guild. Indeed, the painters
of the fifteenth century in Florence, in that gold-
en age of art history, were enrolled in the Guild
of Physicians and Apothecaries. Then, the artist
served a long apprenticeship and labored inter-
minable hours and was bound down in his performance by a rigid contract. And when his work
was done, his fellow townsmen entered the
church or public building to judge it. There was

as yet no Bohemia for the artist, no Gallery for the connoisseurs.

Today the setting is different. It requires a special effort to make contact with art, and the individual who visits museums and galleries for the "previews" and takes tea or cocktails at "openings" labels himself an *art lover* and believes he is thus set apart from ordinary mortals. Yet he is no better endowed to understand or enjoy what he sees than the rest of us even if he peppers his conversation with those art expressions most stylish at the moment. We have on our side that great genius of satire, Hogarth, who wrote that art is accessible to all "however they may have been awed and overborn by pompous terms of art, hard names, etc."

Let almost any "art lover," including the critic, think of the first pictures which enchanted him. He must go far back to memories of childhood no doubt, and then surely his favorites were those pictures which *told stories* . . . graphic, romantic, tender as the case might be. These are the very pictures which he grew up to recognize as second rate or even bad by his new-found standards. But is there no place for these in his new, more austere scheme of things? They served a real purpose when they first awakened his interest. We feel that there is need for more generosity in modern criticism and much more humility. The most overworked cliché in art discussions is the one that goes "I don't know much about Art but I know what I like." Happy the individual for whom this is true! A discerning cartoonist once did a sketch in which a venerable, bearded art critic stands in a salon where the walls are covered with canvases. He is obviously confused. The caption reads "I know *all* about Art, but I don't know what I like."

Let us then take all the definitions and theories and try to discover some central idea common to all. They agree in one major respect—that art is really little more than another man's mode of expressing universal *sentiments, ideas,* or *experiences.* He may have his richest experiences when contemplating the wonders of the physical universe about him, or he might be one to get his stimuli from a world of dreams and from things or adventures imagined. In this respect he is little different from you and me. But he does have a more adequate tool than most of us for expressing what he thinks and feels, and for recording it in at least semipermanent form. If what he has to say is so subtle and his mode of expression so obscure that we do not understand him, then his contribution is a small one and destined to be short-lived.

Now there is another way to make people aware of art. This is the romantic biography. We have all witnessed the phenomenon of the crowds rushing to art exhibits, many never having been inside a museum before, because a novelist had used as his central character a strange painter, Vincent Van Gogh, who in one episode cuts off his ear and sends it as a gift to a prostitute. That ear sent millions into museums! But even here some benefit results. A first exposure to art is thus made. Perhaps the anecdote will recede ultimately to the more distant planes of memory. Perhaps images of the paintings themselves will be recollected by the visitor, and a new and good habit thus acquired.

We return to the thought that Sentiment must return to writing on art. We hold not with the critic who plays the part of a surgeon doing an autopsy. The patient dead, all sentience gone, his is a cold job of analysis. He takes our picture apart and makes his report. We can do that with automobiles and tanks and dishwashers, but not with paintings. We introduce here one disclaimer. We certainly do not feel that all serious art criticism is bad; we have selected two splendid examples for inclusion in this book. We cavil only at that writer who confounds us with phrases that mean nothing, with interpretations that are not valid, and with a generally awesome analysis of shapes, forms, and visions apparent only to himself.

By the same token we do not feel that the reader should deduce that he knows as much as the expert as soon as he begins to look at pictures. We feel that the enjoyment of art comes first and easily, and we emphasize the implications of the word enjoyment. When you see a picture and take pleasure in its contemplation, enjoyment results. We prefer to give to the word appreciation a more elevated connotation. Enjoyment is but a part of it. When we see a painting in terms of the age, the atmosphere, the circumstances which produced it, then we are coming closer to a true appreciation and our experience is bound to be a richer one.

In the field of aesthetics it is simple enough to be a stormy petrel. This is hardly our purpose. We are here interested in good writing and in good Art. It is our hope that the excerpts here reprinted will stimulate readers to seek out the original works of the masters discussed. No criticism or fine writing could ever be a substitute for what will be learned or felt about a work of art when the observer stands before it.

There is one quality common to all the writing in this book. It is personal, subjective, often passionate. These are not writers fearful of admitting that they have strong emotional reactions when looking at a picture or statue. They have a case to plead, a hero to champion. Theirs is not the rôle of judge but rather that of the barrister who will do his best to win his case. Here you will not come upon the careful appraisals of the doctor of philosophy. But on almost every page you will encounter the thoughts and sentiments of gifted men who felt sincerely what they said in whatever medium they used. They will not lead you astray, I am sure. And if they do lead the reader to a better understanding of the masters, the purpose of this volume will be amply fulfilled.

HERMAN J. WECHSLER

THE POCKET BOOK OF
OLD MASTERS

RIGHT: PL. 1

LEONARDO DA VINCI

Self-Portrait

DA VINCI   PL. 2

THE ANNUNCIATION
[DETAIL]

DA VINCI   PL. 3

BEATRICE D'ESTE

DA VINCI   PL. 4

HEAD OF ST. ANNE

[DETAIL]

DA VINCI   PL. 5

MONA LISA

DA VINCI   PL. 6

HEAD OF THE SAVIOR

DA VINCI   PL. 7

THE LAST SUPPER
[DETAIL]

DA VINCI   PL. 8

LA BELLE FERRONNIÈRE

LEONARDO DA VINCI

1452 - 1519

Leonardo da Vinci. *Here indeed is a name to conjure with. Wizard and magician he has been called by his contemporaries and by posterity. His was the most inquiring mind of all time, for he saw mystery everywhere and delved deep to solve it. He studied the earth and the sky. He was one of the first to divine that water had once covered the entire known world. He contemplated the heavens and recorded the movements of stars. He drew plans for flying machines and war-machinery and pipe-lines and cathedrals. He made sketches of the naked body which he cut open himself; he drew the likenesses of the freaks of nature wherever he found them. He drew pictures of saints and madonnas and fauns and pagan folk out of fable and legend.*

It is surprising that Leonardo's extraordinary observations, so many of them revolutionary in theory, did not influence his contemporaries more than history indicates. But it was only at a comparatively late date that his voluminous hand-written manuscripts were deciphered and pub-

lished for an astonished world to contemplate. We can thus skip back over the centuries and examine as no kinsman of his might, the entire range of his prodigious achievement.

The passages of haunting beauty which are quoted in the following pages are from Walter Pater's essay on Leonardo. This essay is but one of a series which comprise the volume published in 1873 under the title Studies in the History of the Renaissance. There is nowhere a more just appraisal of its worth than in these phrases of Arthur Symons, himself a brilliant essayist and critic. He writes, "That book of Studies in the Renaissance, even with the rest of Pater to choose from, seems to me sometimes to be the most beautiful book of prose in our literature."

The original text is here recorded in a somewhat shortened version, but the reader of this chapter will find easy access to the complete volume. Our selection contains passages and images of sheerest poetry revealing keen insight into the mind of one of the few real geniuses of recorded history. And with this rare insight into a unique mind is combined the most subtle appreciation of those few works of Leonardo in the realm of painting which have been preserved.

H. J. W.

LEONARDO DA VINCI

by

Walter Pater

HIS LIFE has three divisions—thirty years at Florence, nearly twenty years at Milan, then nineteen years of wandering, till he sinks to rest under the protection of Francis the First at the *Château de Clou.* The dishonor of illegitimacy hangs over his birth. Piero Antonio, his father, was of a noble Florentine house, of Vinci in the *Val d'Arno,* and Leonardo, brought up delicately among the true children of that house, was the love-child of his youth, with the keen, puissant nature such children often have. We see him in his boyhood fascinating all men by his beauty, improvising music and songs, buying the caged birds and setting them free, as he walked the streets of Florence, fond of odd bright dresses and spirited horses.

From his earliest years he designed many objects, and constructed models in relief, of which Vasari mentions some of women smiling. His father, pondering over this promise in the child, took him to the workshop of Andrea del Verrocchio, then the most famous artist in Florence.

Beautiful objects lay about there—reliquaries, pyxes, silver images for the pope's chapel at Rome, strange fancy-work of the middle age, keeping odd company with fragments of antiquity, then but lately discovered. Another student Leonardo may have seen there—a lad into whose soul the level light and aërial illusions of Italian sunsets had passed, in after days famous as Perugino.

Verrocchio was an artist of the earlier Florentine type, carver, painter, and worker in metals, in one; designer, not of pictures only, but of all things for sacred or household use, drinking-vessels, ambries, instruments of music, making them all fair to look upon, filling the common ways of life with the reflection of some far-off brightness; and years of patience had refined his hand till his work was now sought after from distant places.

It happened that Verrocchio was employed by the brethren of Vallombrosa to paint the Baptism of Christ, and Leonardo was allowed to finish an angel in the left-hand corner. The pupil surpassed the master; and Verrocchio turned away as one stunned, and as if his sweet earlier work must thereafter be distasteful to him, from the bright animated angel of Leonardo's hand.

The angel may still be seen in Florence, a space of sunlight in the cold, labored old picture; but the legend is true only in sentiment, for painting had always been the art by which Verrocchio set least store. And as in a sense he anticipates Leonardo, so to the last Leonardo recalls the studio of Verrocchio. Amid all the cunning and intricacy of his Lombard manner this never left him.

And because it was the perfection of that style, it awoke in Leonardo some seed of discontent which lay in the secret places of his nature. For the way to perfection is through a series of disgusts; and this picture—all that he had done so far in his life at Florence—was after all in the old slight manner. His art, if it was to be something in the world, must be weighted with more of the meaning of nature and purpose of humanity. Nature was "the true mistress of higher intelligences." He plunged, then, into the study of nature. For years he seemed to those about him as one listening to a voice silent for other men.

He learned here the art of going deep, of tracking the sources of expression to their subtlest retreats, the power of an intimate presence in the things he handled. He did not at once or entirely desert his art; only he was no longer the cheerful, objective painter, through whose soul, as through clear glass, the bright figures of Florentine life, only made a little mellower and more pensive by the transit, passed on to the white wall. He wasted many days in curious tricks of design, seeming to lose himself in the spinning of intricate devices of line and color. He was smitten with a love of the impossible—the perforation of mountains, changing the course of rivers, raising great buildings, such as the church of *San Giovanni,* in the air; all those feats for the performance of which natural magic professed to have the key. Later writers, indeed, see in these efforts an anticipation of modern mechanics; in him they were rather dreams, thrown off by the overwrought and laboring brain.

The year 1483—the year of the birth of Raphael and the thirty-first of Leonardo's life—is fixed as the date of his visit to Milan by the letter in which he recommends himself to Ludovico Sforza, and offers to tell him, for a price, strange secrets in the art of war. The fame of Leonardo had gone before him, and he was to model a colossal statue of Francesco, the first Duke of Milan. As for Leonardo himself, he came not as an artist at all, or careful of the fame of one; but as a player on the harp, a strange harp of silver of his own construction, shaped in some curious likeness to a horse's skull. The capricious spirit of Ludovico was susceptible also to the power of music, and Leonardo's nature had a kind of spell in it. Fascination is always the word descriptive of him. No portrait of his youth remains; but all tends to make us believe that up to this time some charm of voice and aspect, strong enough to balance the disadvantage of his birth, had played about him. His physical

6

strength was great; it was said that he could bend a horseshoe like a coil of lead.

The *Duomo,* work of artists from beyond the Alps, so fantastic to the eye of a Florentine used to the mellow, unbroken surfaces of Giotto and Arnolfo, was then in all its freshness; and below, in the streets of Milan, moved a people as fantastic, changeful, and dreamlike.

The movement of the fifteenth century was twofold; partly the Renaissance, partly also the coming of what is called the "modern spirit," with its realism, its appeal to experience. It comprehended a return to antiquity, and a return to nature. Raphael represents the return to antiquity, and Leonardo the return to nature.

In him first appears the taste for what is *bizarre* or *recherché* in landscape; hollow places full of the green shadow of bituminous rocks, ridged reefs of trap-rock which cut the water into quaint sheets of light,—their exact antitype is in our own western seas; all the solemn effects of moving water.

And not into nature only; but he plunged also into human personality, and became above all a painter of portraits; faces of a modelling more skilful than has been seen before or since, embodied with a reality which almost amounts to illusion, on the dark air. To take a character as it was, and delicately sound its stops, suited one so curious in observation, curious in invention. He painted thus the portraits of Ludovico's mistresses, Lucretia Crivelli and Cecilia Galerani the poetess, of Ludovico himself, and the Duchess Beatrice. The portrait of Cecilia Galerani is lost, but that of Lucretia Crivelli has been identified with *La Belle Ferronnière* of the Louvre, and Ludovico's pale, anxious face still remains in the Ambrosian library. Opposite is the portrait of Beatrice d'Este, in whom Leonardo seems to have caught some presentiment of early death, painting her precise and grave, full of the refinement of the dead, in sad earth-colored raiment, set with pale stones.

About the *Last Supper*, its decay and restorations, a whole literature has risen up, Goethe's pensive sketch of its sad fortunes being perhaps the best. The death in childbirth of the Duchess Beatrice was followed in Ludovico by one of those paroxysms of religious feeling which in him were constitutional. The low, gloomy Dominican church of *Saint Mary of the Graces* had been the favorite oratory of Beatrice. She had spent her last days there, full of sinister presentiments; at last it had been almost necessary to remove her from it by force; and now it was here that mass was said a hundred times a day for her repose. On the damp wall of the refectory, oozing with mineral salts, Leonardo painted the *Last Supper*. Effective anecdotes were told about it, his retouchings and delays. They show him re-

8

fusing to work except at the moment of invention, scornful of anyone who supposed that art could be a work of mere industry and rule, often coming the whole length of Milan to give a single touch. He painted it, not in fresco, where all must be *impromptu*, but in oils, the new method which he had been one of the first to welcome, because it allowed of so many afterthoughts, so refined a working out of perfection. It turned out that on a plastered wall no process could have been less durable. Within fifty years it had fallen into decay. And now we have to turn back to Leonardo's own studies, above all to one drawing of the central head at the Brera, which, in a union of tenderness and severity in the face-lines, reminds one of the monumental work of Mino da Fiesole, to trace it as it was.

Here was another effort to lift a given subject out of the range of its traditional associations. Strange, after all the mystic developments of the middle age, was the effort to see the Eucharist, not as the pale Host of the altar, but as one taking leave of his friends. Five years afterwards the young Raphael, at Florence, painted it with sweet and solemn effect in the refectory of Saint Onofrio; but still with all the mystical unreality of the school of Perugino. Vasari pretends that the central head was never finished. But finished or unfinished, or owing part of its effect to a mellowing decay, the head of Jesus does but consummate the sentiment of the whole company—ghosts through which you see the wall, faint as the shadows of the leaves upon the wall on autumn afternoons. This figure is but the faintest, the most spectral of them all.

The *Last Supper* was finished in 1497; in 1498 the French entered Milan, and whether or not the Gascon bowmen used it as a mark for their arrows, the model of Francesco Sforza certainly did not survive. What, in that age, such work was capable of being—of what nobility, amid what racy truthfulness to fact—we may judge from the bronze statue of Bartolomeo Colleoni on horseback, modelled by Leonardo's master, Verrocchio (he died of grief, it was said, because, the mold accidentally failing, he was unable to complete it), still standing in the *piazza* of Saint John and Saint Paul at Venice. Some traces of the thing may remain in certain of Leonardo's drawings, and perhaps also, by a singular circumstance, in a far-off town of France. For Ludovico became a prisoner, and ended his days at Loches in Touraine. After many years of captivity in the dungeons below, where all seems sick with barbarous feudal memories, he was allowed at last, it is said, to breathe fresher air for awhile in one of the rooms of the great tower still shown, its walls covered with strange painted arabesques, ascribed by tradition to his hand, amused a little, in this way, through the tedious years. In those

vast helmets and human faces and pieces of armor, among which, in great letters, the motto
Infelix Sum is woven in and out, it is perhaps not
too fanciful to see the fruit of a wistful after-
dreaming over Leonardo's sundry experiments
on the armed figure of the great duke, which
had occupied the two so much during the days
of their good fortune at Milan.

The remaining years of Leonardo's life are
more or less years of wandering. From his brilliant life at court he had saved nothing, and he
returned to Florence a poor man. Perhaps necessity kept his spirit excited: the next four years
are one prolonged rapture of ecstasy of invention. He painted now the pictures of the Louvre,
his most authentic works, which came there
straight from the cabinet of Francis the First, at
Fontainebleau. One picture of his, the *Saint Anne*
—not the *Saint Anne* of the Louvre, but a simple
cartoon, now in London—revived for a moment
a sort of appreciation more common in an earlier
time, when good pictures had still seemed mi-
raculous. For two days a crowd of people of all
qualities passed in naïve excitement through the
chamber where it hung, and gave Leonardo a
taste of the "triumph" of Cimabue. But his work
was less with the saints than with the living wom-
en of Florence. For he lived still in the polished
society that he loved, and in the houses of Florence, left perhaps a little subject to light thoughts

by the death of Savonarola—the latest gossip (1869) is of an undraped Mona Lisa, found in some out-of-the-way corner of the late *Orleans* collection—he saw Ginevra di Benci, and Lisa, the young third wife of Francesco del Giocondo. As we have seen him using incidents of sacred story, not for their own sake, nor as mere subjects for pictorial realisation, but as a cryptic language for fancies all his own, so now he found a vent for his thought in taking one of these languid women, and raising her, as Leda or Pomona, as Modesty or Vanity, to the seventh heaven of symbolical expression.

La Gioconda is, in the truest sense, Leonardo's masterpiece, the revealing instance of his mode of thought and work. In suggestiveness, only the *Melancholia* of Dürer is comparable to it; and no crude symbolism disturbs the effect of its subdued and graceful mystery. We all know the face and hands of the figure, set in its marble chair, in that circle of fantastic rocks, as in some faint light under sea. Perhaps of all ancient pictures time has chilled it least. As often happens with works in which invention seems to reach its limit, there is an element in it given to, not invented by, the master. In that inestimable folio of drawings, once in the possession of Vasari, were certain designs by Verrocchio, faces of such impressive beauty that Leonardo in his boyhood copied them many times. It is hard not to connect with these designs of the elder, by-past master, as with its germinal principle, the unfathomable smile, always with a touch of something sinister in it, which plays over all Leonardo's work. Besides, the picture is a portrait. From childhood we see this image defining itself on the fabric of his dreams, and but for express historical testimony, we might fancy that this was but his ideal lady, embodied and beheld at last. What was the relationship of a living Florentine to this creature of his thought? By what strange affinities had the dream and the person grown up thus apart, and yet so closely together? Present from the first incorporeally in Leonardo's brain, dimly traced in the designs of Verrocchio, she is found present at last in *Il Giocondo's* house. That there is much of mere portraiture in the picture is attested by the legend that by artificial means, the presence of mimes and flute-players, that subtle expression was protracted on the face. Again, was it in four years and by renewed labor never really completed, or in four months and as by stroke of magic, that the image was projected?

The presence that rose thus so strangely beside the waters, is expressive of what in the ways of a thousand years men had come to desire. Hers is the head upon which all "the ends of the world are come," and the eyelids are a little weary. It is a beauty wrought out from within upon the flesh, the deposit, little cell by cell, of strange thoughts and fantastic reveries and exquisite passions. Set it for a moment beside one of those white Greek goddesses or beautiful women of antiquity, and how would they be troubled by this beauty, into which the soul with all its maladies has passed! All the thoughts and experience of the world have etched and moulded there, in that which they have of power to refine and make expressive the outward form, the animalism of Greece, the lust of Rome, the mysticism of the middle age with its spiritual ambition and imaginative loves, the return of the Pagan world, the sins of the Borgias. She is older than the rocks among which she sits; like the vampire, she has been dead many times, and learned the secrets of the grave; and has been a diver in deep seas, and keeps their fallen day about her; and trafficked for strange webs with Eastern merchants, and, as Leda, was the mother of Helen of Troy, and, as Saint Anne, the mother of Mary; and all this has been to her but as the sound of lyres and flutes, and lives only in the delicacy with which it has moulded the changing lineaments, and tinged the eyelids and the hands. The fancy of a perpetual life, sweeping together ten thousand experiences, is an old one; and modern philosophy has conceived the idea of humanity as wrought upon by, and summoning up in itself, all modes of thought and life. Certainly Lady Lisa might stand as the embodiment of the old fancy, the symbol of the modern idea.

During these years at Florence Leonardo's history is the history of his art; for himself, he is lost in the bright cloud of it.

One other great work was left for him to do, a work all trace of which soon vanished, [a work] in which he had Michelangelo for his rival. Leonardo chose an incident from the battle of Anghiari, in which two parties of soldiers fight for a standard. Like Michelangelo's, his cartoon is lost, and has come to us only in sketches, and in a fragment of Rubens. Michelangelo was twenty-seven years old; Leonardo more than fifty; and Raphael, then nineteen years of age, visiting Florence for the first time, came and watched them as they worked.

We catch a glimpse of Leonardo again, at Rome in 1514, surrounded by his mirrors and vials and furnaces, making strange toys that seemed alive of wax and quicksilver. The hesitation which had haunted him all through life, and made him like one under a spell, was upon him now with double force. No one had ever carried political indifferentism farther; it had always been his philosophy to "fly before the storm"; he is for the Sforzas, or against them, as the tide of their fortune turns. Yet now, in the political society of Rome, he came to be suspected of secret French sympathies. It paralysed him to find himself among enemies; and he turned wholly to France, which had long courted him.

France was about to become an Italy more Italian than Italy itself. Francis the First, like Louis the Twelfth before him, was attracted by the *finesse* of Leonardo's work; *La Gioconda* was already in his cabinet, and he offered Leonardo the little *Château de Clou,* with its vineyards and meadows, in the pleasant valley of the Masse, just outside the walls of the town of Amboise, where, especially in the hunting season, the court then frequently resided. *A Monsieur Lyonard, peinteur du Roy pour Amboyse*—so the letter of Francis the First is headed. It opens a prospect, one of the most interesting in the history of art, where, in a peculiarly blent atmosphere, Italian art dies away as a French exotic.

RIGHT: PL. 9

RAPHAEL SANZIO

Self-Portrait

RAPHAEL   PL. 10

SCHOOL OF ATHENS
[DETAIL]

RAPHAEL

PL. 11

Madonna Del Cardellino

[detail]

RAPHAEL   PL. 12

MADONNA DEL GRANDUCA
[DETAIL]

RIGHT: PL. 13

MICHELANGELO BUONARROTI

PORTRAIT OF THE ARTIST

MICHELANGELO PL. 14

HEAD OF JEHOVA

[DETAIL FROM The Creation]

MICHELANGELO PL. 15

HEAD OF ADAM

[DETAIL FROM The Creation]

MICHELANGELO PL. 16

The Prophet Jeremiah

MICHELANGELO   PL. 17

The Prophet Isaiah

MICHELANGELO   PL. 18

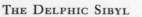

THE DELPHIC SIBYL

MICHELANGELO   PL. 19

The Libyan Sibyl

[DETAIL]

RIGHT: PL. 20

TITIAN

Self-Portrait

TITIAN   PL. 21

ISABELLA OF PORTUGAL

TITIAN   PL. 22

THE DUKE OF NORFOLK

TITIAN   PL. 23

LAVINIA

TITIAN   PL. 24

LAURA DE DIÀNTI

[ALLEGORY]

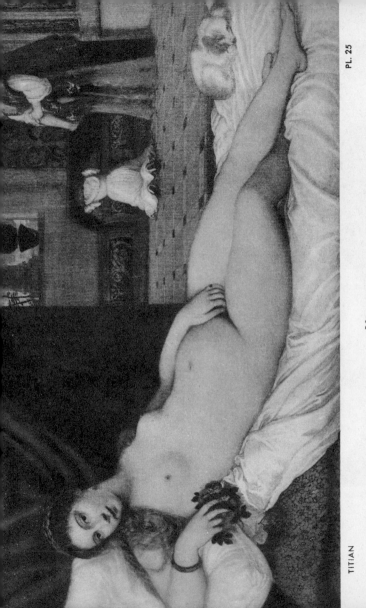

TITIAN

VENUS

RAPHAEL

1483 - 1520

WE HAVE SELECTED *as Raphael's biographer,
the Italian painter, writer and architect, Giorgio
Vasari, who is best known to our age for his colorful, ambitious and often garrulous accounts of
the artists of his own time. It is revealing to see
how a contemporary reacts to and records the life
and achievement of a man he knew and admired.
When Vasari writes of men already dead and
legendary, he is apt to borrow from the realm of
anecdote and colorful story. Admittedly, Vasari
had a real feeling for a tale well told and any unusual yarn was sure to find its way into his pages.
Many writers have based their content on the
chapters of his entertaining work, perpetuating
fictions Vasari invented.*

*But of Raphael, Vasari wrote with assurance,
for here was a man whom he knew, respected
and loved.*

*Of Raphael, the "divine painter," much has
been written. His life, lived fully and picturesque-
ly through its brief span, lends itself readily to
dramatization.*

Handsome of mien, beloved of the fair sex of Umbria, Florence and Rome, he was surrounded by wealth, culture and kingly living. His precocious talent revealed itself as soon as he entered his master's studio at the age of 16. His output was prodigious and his versatility permitted him to change and alter his style whenever he came into contact with the great geniuses whose works he studied in Florence and Rome. Indeed he owes much to Leonardo and Michelangelo.

Raphael is perhaps best known for his highly idealized and ethereal Madonnas. Here is feminine beauty as pure and perfect as mortal man would have it and through many cultures the Raphael type of womanly beauty has continued to reappear. His Saints and Virgins have just enough of the earthly to make them desirable to man, and just enough aloofness to reserve them a place in the ethereal hierarchy. How fleshly and sensuous the young Raphael could be, we may see in his designs for the depiction of the legend of Galatea and of Cupid and Psyche.

But the great Raphael is the painter who furnished the heroic series for the Vatican—"The School of Athens," "Parnassus," and the dramatic "Heliodorus Driven from the Temple." This is the Raphael who takes his place with the other great giants of the golden age in Italy, Leonardo and Michelangelo.

H. J. W.

RAPHAEL

by

Giorgio Vasari

HEAVEN sometimes showers infinite riches on
one sole favorite—treasures which are usually dis-
tributed over a long period of time and among
many individuals. This is clearly shown in the
case of Raphael Sanzio of Urbino. As excellent
as he was graceful, Raphael was modest and
good. Gentle and always ready to conciliate, he
was considerate of everyone. At the moment
when nature was vanquished by the art of
Michelangelo, she deigned to be subjugated by
Raphael, who combined art and nature. Till then,
artists often had been rude, eccentric, uncouth,
or fantastic, sometimes even stained by vice. In
Raphael the rarest qualities of the heart shone
forth; his character was perfected by diffidence,
application to study, and an excellence of life
that was quite exceptional. We may not call such
men as Raphael common men. They are rather
mortal gods who leave such fame on earth that
they may hope for sure rewards in heaven here-
after.

Raphael was born at Urbino, that renowned

city, on Good Friday, 1483, at nine o'clock at night. His father was Giovanni de' Santi, a painter of no great eminence, but an intelligent and cultivated man. He insisted that his son should not be given to a wet nurse, but be nourished by his own mother. He also desired to bring up his own child rather than let him be sent where he might learn unrefined habits and manners. As the child grew older, Giovanni began to instruct him in the first principles of painting.

At length, Giovanni realized that he was not able to teach his son as he should be taught. This good and kind parent resolved to place the boy with Pietro Perugino, who was considered the first painter of his time. Giovanni went to Perugia but found Pietro absent from the city. While he waited for him, Giovanni painted certain works for the church of San Francesco. After Pietro returned, Giovanni made his acquaintance, and when the opportunity presented itself, made his request in the most suitable manner. Pietro, with equal courtesy, agreed to accept the care of Raphael. So Giovanni went back to Urbino to fetch the boy. Raphael's departure for Perugia was not made without many tears from his devoted mother. As soon as Pietro saw Raphael's drawings and his pleasing deportment, he conceived that opinion of him which was in time so amply confirmed.

While he studied with Perugino, Raphael imitated his master's manner so exactly that one cannot tell their works apart. This is proved by an Assumption in San Francesco at Perugia. Anyone would take it for a Perugino, but it is certainly a Raphael. In Città di Castello Raphael painted several pictures which, were it not for his signature, would certainly be supposed to be by Perugino.

While Raphael was earning fame by these labors, Pinturicchio, a friend of his, was commissioned to paint the library of Pius II in Siena. He took Raphael along with him. Raphael made some of the cartoons for the decorations and would have continued to work there had he not heard reports of Leonardo's cartoon for the great hall of the palace in Florence and the cartoon of the *Nude Bathers* by Michelangelo Buonarroti. Fired by the desire to see these drawings, Raphael set aside his own interests and convenience and at once proceeded to Florence.

While in Florence, this most excellent painter studied the ancient works of Masaccio. This and what he saw in the work of Leonardo and Michelangelo helped him to make great progress in art. He formed a close intimacy with Fra Bartolommeo di San Marco and imitated his coloring. He, for his part, taught the good father the rules of perspective, to which the monk had not previously given his attention.

Raphael left Florence because Bramante of

Urbino, who was then in the service of Pope Julius II and who was a remote kinsman as well as a fellow townsman of Raphael's, wrote to say that he had persuaded the Pope to entrust Raphael with the decoration of some new rooms in the Vatican. Gratified by this proposal, he left his works in Florence unfinished and proceeded to Rome. There he found many of the rooms already painted, or in the process of being painted, by different masters. For example, there was a historical picture by Piero della Francesco, and one side of another room had a painting by Luca da Cortona [Signorelli], and there were others.

Pope Julius received Raphael with much kindness. Raphael began a picture, in the chamber of the Segnatura, of the reconciliation of Philosophy and Astrology with Theology [the *School of Athens*]. The composition is so perfect in every part that the master proved his supremacy over all painters. The whole was finished in a manner so delicate and harmonious that Pope Julius resolved that the other pictures, old or new, should be destroyed at once, and that Raphael alone should have the glory of seeing his work preferred above all others.

Raphael, famous as he was, and familiar with the antique, had not yet formed his grand style. One day Bramante, who had a key, let him in to see the unfinished Sistine Chapel, while Michelangelo was absent in Florence. Instantly, Raphael repainted the figure of the prophet Isaiah, which he had finished in the church of San Agostino, and in this work he profited so greatly by what he had seen in the work of Michelangelo that his manner was inexpressibly enlarged and received henceforth an obvious increase in majesty.

But when Michelangelo afterward saw the work of Raphael, he thought that Bramante had wronged him in order to enhance Raphael's fame.

Soon after this, Agostino Chigi, a very rich merchant of Siena, gave Raphael a commission to paint a chapel, because the master had recently done a fresco of Galatea in a loggia of his palace [the Farnesina] showing the nymph drawn by dolphins and surrounded by tritons. The chapel is in the church of Santa Maria del Pace, on the right as you enter. Raphael painted it in his new manner and put in it some of the prophets and sibyls before Michelangelo had thrown open the Sistine Chapel. These figures are considered to be the best, and among so many beautiful, the most beautiful that Raphael ever executed.

His fame and the rewards conferred on him increasing largely, Raphael built a palace in the Borgo Nuovo which was decorated with stucco work by Bramante. His renown had reached France and Flanders, and Albrecht Dürer, a most admirable German painter and the engraver of the most beautiful copperplates, sent a tribute of respect to Raphael. It was Dürer's own portrait drawn on very fine linen, so that the drawing showed on both sides. The lights were transparent and painted in water color. Raphael then sent to Dürer a number of his own drawings.

Dürer's engraving prompted Raphael to have his own works engraved by Marcantonio Raimondi of Bologna. It was such a success that Raphael commissioned him to engrave many of his earlier works. A number of these engravings were given by Raphael to his disciple, Il Baviera, who was the guardian of a certain lady to whom Raphael was attached until the day of his death. He painted her portrait to the very life [*La Donna Velata?*]. It is now treasured as a relic for the love he bears to art and most especially to Raphael, by the good and worthy Botti, a merchant of Florence.

Raphael went on with the work in the Vatican, painting, ornamenting, and designing stairways and loggias. He was placed in charge of all the works that were to be executed in the palace. It is said that Raphael was so courteous and obliging that he had the masons leave apertures and spaces for storage room, for the convenience of certain friends. But these spaces weakened the walls and have since had to be filled in.

He designed several palaces, some in Rome and some in Florence.

Raphael painted many pictures to be sent into France, one particularly, for King Francis I: a Saint Michael in combat with the archfiend [Louvre, Paris]. The work was performed so admirably at all points that Raphael obtained the large reward he merited. He also painted the portrait of Beatrice of Ferrara and of other ladies, his own inamorata especially.

Raphael was much disposed to the gentler affections and delighted in the society of women. He permitted himself to indulge too freely in the pleasures of life. We find it related that his intimate friend, Agostino Chigi, commissioned him to paint the first floor of his palace, but Raphael was so engrossed in his love for the lady of his choice that Agostino, in despair of seeing the work finished, prevailed upon the lady to come and live in his house. Then the work was at last brought to a conclusion.

I must say something about Raphael's style for the benefit of those who practice our calling, before I tell what remains to be told about his life. As a child, he imitated Perugino but improved upon him in every way. Then, when he saw the work of Leonardo, he set himself to study it with the utmost zeal, for it pleased him more than anything he had ever seen. But whatever he did, and in spite of his best endeavor, he could not surpass that master. Many think Raphael surpassed Leonardo in tenderness and in a certain natural facility, but he was surely by no means superior in that force of conception which is so noble a foundation of art, and in which few masters have equaled Leonardo. Raphael had drawn from the nude only after the manner of Perugino and found himself unable to master the freedom of Michelangelo, as shown in the cartoon in the Hall of the Council. After having been a master, he became again a disciple and compelled himself to learn in a few months what would have taken years of boyhood. He devoted himself to the study of anatomy by dissecting and studying the articulation of the bones and the muscles, the sinews, the nerves, and the veins. He knew, nevertheless, that he could never equal Michelangelo, but he considered, like the sensible man he was, that painting does not embrace merely the nude, but has a much wider field. He saw that he who could express a thought clearly and compose without confusion may also be reputed an able master. Raphael rightly thought that art should be enriched by inventions in perspective, by landscapes, and by the skillful use of light and shadow. He learned also from Fra Bartolommeo a grace of design and coloring.

I have thought proper to make these remarks at the close of his life to show to what labor, study, and care this artist subjected himself.

I will now return to the life and death of Raphael. Cardinal Bibbiena, Raphael's intimate friend,

wished the master to marry. Raphael did not re-
fuse, but he put the matter off. At last he accepted Bibbiena's niece, but he continued to put
off the marriage from time to time. His motive
was an honorable one. For Leo X, so they inti-
mated, intended to reward him for his labors
and honor his talents by bestowing upon him
the red hat. The painter, in the meantime, did
not abandon the light attachment by which he
was enchained. One day, returning from one of
these secret visits, he fell ill of a violent fever
which was mistaken for a cold. The doctors bled
him, which exhausted him at the very time when
he needed to be strengthened. Thereupon he
made his will, and like a good Christian he sent
his love from the house, but left her enough to
live on, and divided his property among his disciples. He then confessed, and in much contri-
tion, completed the course of his life on the day
whereon it had commenced, which was Good
Friday. The master was then thirty-seven, and,
as he embellished the world by his talents, so it
is to be believed that his soul is now adorning
heaven.

MICHELANGELO

1475 - 1564

POETS, HISTORIANS, CRITICS, NOVELISTS *have all had occasion to write of and about that giant among giants, Michelangelo Buonarroti. His was a life of which legends are made. A man of tempestuous moods and godlike yearnings he sought to achieve the impossible and came as near to it as any mortal man. His tragedy was the growing realization that he was destined to complete but fragments of the colossal designs that he imagined, planned, and all but brought into heroic being. Indeed, if any man succeeded in making the fragment heroic, it was this Renaissance artist whose life was spent in torment and self-torture. His poetry, his letters, his painting and his sculpture all breathe that "terrible" quality which generations of observers have noted.*

We feel compelled to call attention here to the magnificent appreciation of Michelangelo by Romain Rolland, a writer who understood the tortured genius and comprehended how vast was his influence on his own age and that which fol-

lowed. In the introduction to his book Michel-angelo, *Rolland has this to say:*

"*Nothing like Michelangelo had ever appeared before. . . . Even after he had been gone for a long time, the world of art was still whirled along in the eddies of his wild spirit. Michelangelo captured painting, sculpture, architecture and poetry, all at once; he breathed into them the frenzy of his vigour and of his overwhelming idealism. No one understood him, yet all imitated him.*"

We have chosen for our critic of the life and work of Michelangelo, the Count de Gobineau, who in a masterpiece of imaginative writing has caught as much of the flavor of the Italian Renaissance as any writer in any language. The form he has used for his picturization of Italy of the fifteenth and sixteenth centuries is a dramatic one. The book is composed of playlets, with settings described in theatrical terms. Across these endless stages stride the colorful characters of the period—artists, popes, courtesans and poets.

One of the most poignant scenes in the entire work is that which follows. Michelangelo, working late at night, learns that the youthful Raphael has just died. His soliloquy as imagined by Gobineau, as he remains bemused in his studio and prophesies the twilight descending on Italy and Italian Art, is romantic biography at its very best.

H. J. W.

MICHELANGELO

by

Arthur, Count de Gobineau

A cold and dark retreat. The night is black. A statue, still almost in the rough, on which falls the light of a little copper lamp, held by Antonio Urbino, the artist's servant.

MICHELANGELO: I have not been so happy for many a long day. It is a black night, and by the gleam of this little lamp I see a world of ideas. . . . What may the time be?

URBINO: I think it cannot be far from midnight. You had better go to bed.

MICHELANGELO: It is pouring with rain. One can hear the shower smiting the roofs and falling on the flagstones of the courtyard like a great river. It has been a fearful storm. Lightnings furrow the shimmering blackness of the windowpane. But behind all this stern uproar, what calm! The distant rumblings of the thunder and its majestic roarings, but no human voice, no false, lying, peevish, imperious or stupidly arrogant voice is raised to vex me! I can create . . . my spirit is free . . . I am happy! . . . I am wholly in the power of all that is worth my entire devotion, and the hard bosom of the marble opens . . . the living head begins to appear. . . . White, white, it palpitates beneath the chisel that sets free its features one by one. . . . Out of the material they spring . . . they speak. . . . Urbino!

URBINO: Master?

MICHELANGELO: You are falling asleep on your footstool. It is you who would do well to go and seek your bed.

URBINO: I cannot. When you sleep, I will sleep —not before.

MICHELANGELO: Strange obstinacy!

URBINO: True, I am no longer young, and it wearies me to stay up, but the Marchioness said to me: "When your master does not go to rest, do not go to rest either, and we shall see if he cares to tax the strength of his old servant."

MICHELANGELO: Give me a few minutes more; there is one thing to be finished.

URBINO: A few minutes, but not more. The Marchioness expressly desires . . .

MICHELANGELO: Very well then! . . . Tell me a story to keep me awake.

URBINO: I went to-day to your notary.

MICHELANGELO: We won't speak of that.

URBINO: He says that the two girls whom you have dowered are quite respectable.

MICHELANGELO: I am glad, Urbino. I wish them all happiness; they are lovable children, though very ugly.

URBINO: I also saw your nephew. He came while you were out.

MICHELANGELO: Good. . . . If he should happen to come back, tell him to leave me in peace and go about his business.

URBINO: He thinks, and that rightly, that his most pressing business is to thank you for the three thousand crowns which you, who are not rich, have given him.

MICHELANGELO: He knows that I love him; he has no need to thank me.

URBINO: Master, the clock strikes . . . an hour after midnight. . . .

MICHELANGELO: I have finished . . . but I am mortally hungry. Have you nothing to eat here? Look in the meal-tub.

URBINO: I will go and see. . . . Ah! your house is kept on a poor footing indeed! As soon as you have money, it is given to the first comer.

MICHELANGELO: Man needs but little for his body. But all his strength is insufficient to elevate his soul.

URBINO: Here's some bread . . . a trifle hard . . . and a piece of cheese, and even the end of a bottle. . . .

MICHELANGELO: Excellent! Bring me all that.

Takes off his cardboard cap, puts the lamp on a bench and eats, standing up, looking at his statue. Loud knocking at the door.

Who can be coming at this hour? Look through the grill.

URBINO: Who is knocking?

A VOICE: It is I, Antonio Mini. . . . Open, master! . . . It is I, your pupil! I have important news for you!

MICHELANGELO: My pupil, Antonio Mini? Open! Is it bad tidings?

ANTONIO MINI *(entering):* Oh, master, a terrible misfortune!

MICHELANGELO: What is the matter? You are quite pale!

MINI: Raphael is dying! No doubt he is dead by now.

MICHELANGELO: Raphael! God in heaven!

MINI: I was in his studio with two of his pupils, Timoteo Viti and Il Garofalo. It was about three o'clock. A servant came to say that the master was ill. He had had fever since yesterday evening.

MICHELANGELO: Since yesterday? I am not surprised. He was a man of delicate complexion, half woman, half child. He spent too much time at work and far too much at his pleasures. I met him, four days ago, making excavations in

the Campo Vaccino, and I even remember
warning him to beware of digging at this season of the year. You say he is worse?

MINI: If he is not dead now, he will not last
out till daybreak. He had himself carried into
his studio, and I saw him, yes, I saw him, white
as a shroud, half-fainting, his eyes fixed on his
picture of the Transfiguration. . . . Near the
bed, which had been set up for him in a hurry,
stood his friends, Cardinals Bibbiena, Sadoleto
and Bembo, and other Signors whom I do not
know. . . . At the pillow-side was the Holy
Father, crying and wiping his eyes.

MICHELANGELO: Urbino, give me my cap and
cloak. I must go there! Raphael . . . Raphael
. . . dying! My God, is it possible? . . . Quick,
let us go!

URBINO: Here, here, master! Give me time to
light a lantern; I will light your way.

MICHELANGELO: You say there is no help for it?
Are you certain? Have the physicians been
sent for? What did they say? What did they
do? Let us go!

MINI: There was no lack of physicians; there
was the Holy Father's, Messer Jacopo of Bres-
cia, then Messer Gaëtano Marini, and others.
All looked very gloomy and shook their heads;
their eyes told us that their science could do
no more.

MICHELANGELO: Come, Urbino, are you ready?

URBINO: Here I am, master!

MICHELANGELO: Walk in front, quickly!

They go out into the street, which is very dark; however, the rain has ceased falling; the clouds, rapidly rolled upon one another by the wind, are torn asunder and show a part of the orb of the moon, which gives a faint light to the houses and the road. A great noise of footsteps is heard.

What is this uproar?

URBINO: We shall know after turning the corner of the lane!

MINI: Forward! Mind that puddle of water, master!

He supports Michelangelo by the arm.

Rapidly and confusedly, there passes a numerous company of officers, soldiers, servants and torch-bearers, whose torches throw a red light on the houses; in the midst of this procession, the pontifical litter with curtains drawn.

MICHELANGELO (to a chamberlain): What means this, Sir?

CHAMBERLAIN: It is the Holy Father returning to the Vatican.

MICHELANGELO: Is Raphael . . . ?

A VOICE: Raphael is dead, and Michelangelo alone remains in Italy!

The procession passes; Michelangelo drops on to a stone bench. The clouds have parted, and the moon shines in a clear sky.

MICHELANGELO: I remain, it is true . . . I alone remain. Last year it was Lionardo . . . now it is Raphael, and all whom we three knew or listened to have long since gone. It is true, I alone remain. There was a time when I should have loved to be the only one, the peerless, the unique, the greatest confidant of the secrets of creative heaven! I imagined that to resemble the sun, in the centre of the universe, without an equal, without a rival, was the most enviable form of happiness. . . . For years I was not fond of Lionardo. . . . I railed at Raphael in the bottom of my heart. . . . I repeated to myself, so as to convince myself, that I rated them low. . . . Yes, there have been days when you, Michelangelo, were only a poor creature, of short sight and circumscribed vision, apt to censure and misunderstand all that did not resemble you, and—I tell you, because it is true—all that was quite as good as you and perhaps better! Now I have what my heart desired. The stars have gone out in heaven, and here I am alone . . . quite alone . . . and stifled in my isolation! . . . There is still Titian; he is a great genius, a great brain. . . . There is Andrea del Sarto. . . . There is . . . But, alas! no—great as they are, they are not the peers of Lionardo and of him who lies down there. . . . Ah, Raphael! . . . His beauty, his subtlety, his sweetness, his grace, and, in his talk as in his aspect, what divine honey! . . . all that I have not, all that I cannot reach . . . all that I am not! . . . He whom all loved and who deserved so well to be loved . . . My God, my God, what is it that comes over me? What is stirring within me and drawing tears from eyes that never tried to weep? Of what am I thinking? Yes, a river of grief is rising and rolling within my bosom; the tears escape from my eyelids, stream down my cheeks, fall upon him whom I always abused and shunned, and who was so much better and more loved of Heaven than I! She told me so, she . . . Vittoria . . . she always told me so, and I would not agree. . . . But I know it well, at bottom, I felt it, and now that the thunderbolt of death has passed between him and me, now that I remain here, my feet in the mud of the world, while his noble and charming countenance appears to me in the bosom of God, shining with celestial light, I see how insincere and petty I have been! No . . . no, Titian and the others, however admirable they may be, are not the equals of these two great departed. About them, and about me who remain, the light is waning and receding, the shadows are lengthening. . . . Yes, here I am alone, and the icy breath of the tomb that is opening strikes my face. What will become of the arts? And we, who have hoped so much, desired so much, imagined so much, worked so much, what have we achieved, what shall we bequeath to them that come after us? Not a quarter of what we should have done.

Covers his face with his hands.

URBINO: Come, master, you will take cold.

MINI: Give me your arm, and let us go back to your house.

MICHELANGELO: Yes; we must preserve our strength and work as long as we are throttled by the chain of life.

TITIAN

1477 - 1576

THE ACHIEVEMENT *of Elie Faure in producing his four-volume* History of Art *seems almost as heroic as the performance of Titian himself. Few writers would have dared to undertake so herculean a task as the consideration of all of art history, from its dawning to the present day. Faure's scientific training as a physician may have equipped him in part for so daring an enterprise, but it was the poet in him that helped bring it to fruition. As a "dreamer of dreams" he envisaged the possibility of seeing the whole of man's artistic accomplishment, to record it, and to evaluate it for us.*

Walter Pach, who translated the entire work from the French, has said of Elie Faure, "Only one who feels the emotions of art can tell others which are the great works and make clear the collective poem formed by their history."

Significantly the very opening sentence of the first edition of Faure's work reads "Art, which expresses life, is as mysterious as life. It escapes all formulas, as life does." Challenged by this thought he then attempts to find for us some common equation for a universal understanding of the mystery.

Faure's History of Art *is certainly the most passionate art history ever written. Here is a man who brings strong emotion to every appraisal he makes. He is a coiner of phrases as might be expected of a poet; you may not agree with all that he says, but you will not forget it!*

It is fitting, therefore, that Elie Faure offer here his portrait of Venice and of Titian, one of its more famous sons. As will be seen immediately in the passage which follows, the author first sets the stage with a description of the city itself. Venice, "bride of the Adriatic," city of oriental splendor, is the backdrop against which this "grand old man of painting" is made to move. For a dispassionate appraisal of Titian the man, we may have to look to other pages than these. We recommend the letters he wrote to his contemporary, Pietro Aretino, for an insight into his character. We also suggest Thomas Craven's chapter in his Men of Art *for a realistic consideration of the Venetian in a brilliant thumb-nail sketch. But for an exciting presentation of Titian's art we need look no further than the passage below. Here we have a veritable prose poem with image piling on image to produce a picture as rich with color and movement as the paintings themselves.*

H. J. W.

TITIAN

by

Elie Faure

Titian has painted universal life. When he listens to its voices, one would say that he was indifferent. They all enter into him with equal rights; the bodies of children, the flesh of women, virile faces, gorgeous or sober costumes, architecture, the earth with its trees and its flowers, the sea, the sky, and all the wandering atoms which make it impossible for the sea and the sky to cease combining their forces. Creative enthusiasm raises him to such a height that his serenity does not desert him even when this entire world, assimilated and recreated in a new order, issues from him in waves continually increasing in length and breadth. He organizes his world into symphonies in which everything that is human resounds in uninterrupted echoes through everything that lives with an instinctive and obscure life, where everything that is material penetrates the human forms and fuses with them for eternity.

In Venice one no longer finds detached edges in the diamond of the atmosphere, there are no

more of those imperious lines cutting out the hills
and the graded terraces against the sky. There is
nothing but the space in which objects tremble,
combine, and became dissociated; a world of reflections, modified, inverted, suppressed, or renewed repeatedly by the hours of the day and
by the seasons. On the palaces, red-brown or
purple, or covered with a crust of musty gold, all
the colors of the prism are awakened, are ef-
faced, come to light again, and prolong themselves as if drawn out in thick strokes. The mirror
of the sea casts its reflections into the vapors
that arise from it under the downpour of light,
and when these vapors pass in clouds over the
glistening canals, the sky throws back thick shadows upon them and reflects the airy phantom of
the waters.

All the painting of Titian is here, and after it
all the painting of Venice, and after the painting
of Venice all the painting that has life, which sees
colors penetrating one another, reflections play-
ing upon surfaces, transparent shadows taking on
color—painting in which no tone is ever repeated
in the same manner, but dominates by discreetly
reminding one of itself, thereby awakening in the
eye the vibration of neighboring hues, the lumi-
nous life of the world, creating a spontaneous
symphony not one beat of which will be born of
matter without our being able to discover the
cause of it and to seek its effect in the whole of

its extent. Doubtless, the discipline gained from the work of Mantegna, later on the influence of Rome, and above all the sensuality which led them necessarily to discover form, the form full and circular which we invariably discover at the conclusion of an investigation into plastics, caused the Venetian painters to see everything gravitating around the volumes which alone are capable of giving us a durable and solid image of the world of our senses. But the Venetians never attained sculptural expression, and Sansovino, their sculptor, who came, however, from Florence, even developed among them a conception of form which, in its shading, vagueness, and grandeur approached that of their painting.

Titian always stops at the instant when, at the edges of the mass that turns before him to vanish in the distant plains, he observes the quivering caress of the atmosphere which, by the gradation of its values, unifies the mass with the volumes of the forests, the clouds, the mountains perceived in the distance. Line has disappeared. The spots of color graded down evoke form sufficiently for it to participate in the life of all space. So the continuity which gives life to the work is no longer found in that inner instinct for social solidarity which, for the artists of the Middle Ages, held things together by invisible bonds; neither is it found in the intellectual arabesque which defined this unity for the mind rather than for the senses: it is in the mutual dependence of all the elements of the world, the forms, the lines, the colors, and the air that unites them; and if, among the Venetians, the moral sentiment seems to efface itself from life, it is to allow the rise, in an irresistible explosion, of the sensual sentiment of the whole body of nature which Christianity had forgotten. Titian not only prevented the original sin of breaking through the symbolic frontiers within which Michelangelo had inclosed it once more, but, by bringing about a more perfect unity in the infinite complexity of all the relationships whose logical interweaving makes a harmonious and living universe, he finished the work of Masaccio, completed that of Bellini, consecrated that of Giorgione, and, before Rabelais, before Shakespeare, before Rubens, before Velasquez and Rembrandt, and long before the German musicians, he announced the modern spirit. He created the symphony. He is the father of painting.

The aristocratic nature inherited from his noble ancestors had been tempered by the elementary force of the country where he was born, at the foot of the Tyrolean Alps, among the lakes and the beech forests above which rises the rampart of the pink Dolomite peaks. Cima da Conegliano had had before his eyes the same mountain landscapes, the same transparent skies, and the blue waters in which sleep the silhouettes of the forti-

fied castles, and when he painted the delicate
altar pictures whose clearly defined figures recall
his master Giovanni Bellini less than they do
Mantegna, he supplied from his own mind scarcely more than the subtle frame, aerial and poetic,
which he purposed to give them. Titian, who was
less than twenty years younger, certainly knew
him and studied him, and sought in his work the
confirmation of his own presentiments. Later on,
whenever he left Venice—and he departed frequently, especially after the descent of Charles
the Fifth upon Italy—he carried with him his
sense of space trembling from molecular vibration, and when, on his travels, he found himself
among lakes, woods, and plains sown with low
cottages and clusters of green oaks, he felt the
confused poetry of the earth as it had never been
felt before.

Thenceforward, space enveloped with its
waves the pagan poems with which he was over-
flowing. The beautiful mature bodies of the Venetian courtesans were displayed before him on
broad beds, wearing only a necklace about their
throats, and holding a tuft of roses in the hollow
of their hands, or they lay under the trees before
a kneeling faun; and the beautiful, mature bodies
glowed with the same serenity that he had found
in the earth. They were waiting. Love was for
them a thing accepted unaffectedly, filled with a
tranquil intoxication, without disquietude or re-

morse. Their eyes were the calm eyes of animals, in which swim the russet reflections of their heavy hair and of the space gathering around them which envelops them in amber. Their breasts rose and fell slowly, their bellies had waves of muscles which merge in the angle of shadow formed by the broad thighs as they come together. With his brush Titian amassed the heavy atmosphere in order to knead it with the substance of the soil, the pulp of the fruits, and the sap of the oaks. And with it all he mingled that winelike purple dipped in gold, which is like a triumphal background for the Venetian apotheosis, which weighs on the shoulders of the bishops in the penumbra flaming within the churches, which dyes the robes of the Doges, unfurls itself from the top of masts and balconies and floats behind the gondolas, which shimmers on façades, stains the walls and floors in the halls of the Ducal Palace with blood as if it were rising through the pores of the stone dungeons below where the Council of Ten caused its decrees to be executed, fills the twilights, trembles in the reflections of the lanterns at the evening water-festivals, and which the sails of ships trail over the sea.

When Titian abandoned that impassive sensual idealism which was the dominating force of his activity, he discovered in the somber purple, lit up by golden spangles, and tempered by fire and sulphur, a powerful and tragic atmosphere, enabling him to enter the human drama with the decision and vigor of which only a great spirit is capable, a spirit which continued to grow up to his hundredth year. It is that bloody light shed by the flickering torches which brings out of the shadow, where the executioners torture Him, that terrible *Christ Crowned with Thorns,* painted, as was the *Pieta,* one of the most melancholy and human works in the history of painting, when he was more than ninety-five—a painting in which there was a premonition of the genius of Rembrandt. It is this bloody light which rises with the dawn and streaks the black iron armor of Charles the Fifth as he comes forth from a black wood, his livid countenance touched by red reflections as he bestrides a black horse caparisoned with red—a horrible symphony of murder, a painting of night and of blood.

Thus there were two directions to his nature which parted at the common center of his limitless receptivity and of his acceptance of life; to organize themselves into vast sensual poems, or to scrutinize the moral world with a cruelty as impassable as his lyricism had seemed. There are no portraits, in Italy or elsewhere, which surpass his. They have that power of defining character which caused the Florentines to produce such terrible effigies, concentrated, nervous, frenzied, and cut out in the mold of passion. Only, these are draped with decorative fullness and searched out with a tranquil penetration unknown to Florence. The fever that consumed her painters no longer exists in Titian. He can paint with a sincerity so uncompromising that it leaves to the Cæsars and to the popes their malformed skulls, their atrophied masks, their jaws of beasts, and their hideous and low mien; he can describe those black-garbed silhouettes, those muscular hands that clutch the hilts of swords, and those pale countenances with haggard eyes, all those violent men made for murder as women are made for love. It is the period in which the *Condottiere* holds Italy in his grasp, when Machiavelli writes *The Prince*. Titian's heads summarize all Italy, from the ferocious portraits of Antonello da Messina who had brought to Venice the oil paintings of the Flemings, and from the tightly drawn faces of Giovanni Bellini to the broad, somewhat soft effigies of that fine painter Paris Bordone, and to the great figures of the Doges which momentarily arrested the disordered, gorgeous, and brutal vision of Tintoretto.

RIGHT: PL. 26

PIETER BRUEGEL THE ELDER

48]   SELF-PORTRAIT

BRUEGEL

THE WEDDING FEAST

BRUEGEL

The Peasant Dance

BRUEGEL

CHILDREN'S GAMES

BRUEGEL

The Harvesters — Summer

BRUEGEL   PL. 31

The Hay Makers
[DETAIL]

RIGHT: PL. 32

PETER PAUL RUBENS
Self-Portrait

RUBENS   PL. 33

The Artist's Children

[detail]

RUBENS   PL. 34

The Judgment of Paris

[detail]

RUBENS   PL. 35

Return of Diana

RIGHT: PL. 36

REMBRANDT VAN RIJN

Self-Portrait

MAN WITH GOLDEN HELMET

REMBRANDT   PL. 38

YOUNG GIRL AT AN OPEN HALF-DOOR

REMBRANDT

THE SYNDICS

REMBRANDT

THE NIGHTWATCH

REMBRANDT

PL. 41

The Admiral's Wife

PIETER BRUEGEL THE ELDER

1525 - 1569

IN VIRGIL BARKER'S STUDY *of the paintings of Pieter Bruegel The Elder, we have the superb combination of fine scholarship, imaginative interpretation and poetic statement. As pointed out by Mr. Barker, it has always been difficult to arrive at a true appraisal of the artist as a man. The legend which has grown up around him derives mainly from a work by Carel Van Mander who published his* The Book of the Painters *some thirty years after Bruegel's death. Many of his paintings and engravings depict demons and goblins, a fact which accounts for the appellation, Pieter the Droll.*

In Virgil Barker's treatment, however, we begin to have a more complete portrait of the man as seen through his work. His independence is evidenced by the fact that he could go to Italy when Michelangelo and Titian were still at work and come back to Antwerp uninfluenced by what he saw. And Mr. Barker penetrates the apparent grossness of Bruegel and sees in his paintings much more than a simple realistic recording of drunken wild-eyed peasants engaged in revelry and play. He finds rather a keen, sympathetic, and sensitive artist who, intrigued with the costumes, the customs, the superstitions, the folk lore of his own people, endeavors to record all this with his brush and engraver's tool. Bruegel came more and more to identify himself with these peasants and without condescension he makes his paintings humanitarian observations of their way of life.

More than any other scholar who has written of this strange master, Virgil Barker makes us see him against the background of his own time. He explains Bruegel's formation as a thinker and observer, on the basis of the history of his period.

For long years Bruegel was ignored by critics, but today there is probably no "old master" more in vogue. Modern artists claim him as a kindred spirit. I think this is true because he comes closer to achieving what so many of them seek to do. A sentence out of Mr. Barker's piece expresses this perfectly; he says that Bruegel "was interested less in telling what a specific place looked like than in rendering the emotional effect of nature upon himself." When an artist succeeds in conveying to the observer the same emotional reaction he himself has experienced, his work is indeed well done.

H. J. W.

PIETER BRUEGEL THE ELDER

by

Virgil Barker

THE SUBJECT-MATTER of Bruegel's great paintings is limited only by the world and life. The
whole cycle of nature is in them—the seasons as
they pass over mountain, plain and moving waters; the dazzling beauty of the southern sea, the
northern cold. The entire range of human life is
in them; somewhere in these multitudes every
emotion finds its expressive gesture. Even all the
animals that are intimately a part of human life
are given in their degrees of individuality. These
pictures seem to set before the eye every experience possible to man.

In Bruegel's time story-telling in pictures generally was still one of the principal means of
communicating ideas—even, perhaps mainly,
ideas that were not inherently pictorial; prints
were still the nearest things to books in popular
circulation. Moreover, a nation living under the
necessity of never speaking out openly on either
politics or religion naturally resorted to symbol,
the concrete proverb or the image that said one
thing and meant another. The print of the big

and little fish not only meant that the great oppressed the small but carried an idea beyond the words of the proverb in showing the big fish ripped up and disgorging; and upon a people so apt at interpreting images the significance of that would not be lost. This people could not only take a hearty enjoyment of the good things of life but they could also face the whole of it without shrinking from any part of it, whether of grossness or of terror. For the latter, indeed, they even had a gusto and the former they laughed away with a saving healthiness. The distinguishing mark of their living and their thinking was a robust realism.

In Pieter Bruegel there emerged from among them a man of genius in complete sympathy with their realistic attitude towards life; knowing it from childhood, he gave it in his art a more complete expression than it had ever had before. The whole originality and fertility of his mind were for long expended upon feeding the popular taste not only for the familiar or exotic beauty of nature but also for a rough philosophy, unorganized but none the less genuine; and a habit so well established in him by years of labor would not vanish all at once even when more purely painter-like interests assumed for him a major importance. His predecessors in painting had been realistic in their measure; in them, however, realism was largely confined to details of execution and was more than counterbalanced by markedly idealistic conceptions.

To examine the *Proverbs* in detail is to get a feeling of being among mad folks because so many of the sayings here illustrated turn upon outlandish actions; but as a picture it is a piece of masterly realistic sanity showing a whole village, in which some of the inhabitants happen to be crazy, intensely busy about its own affairs. The *Triumph of Death*, so far from being a piece of wild and gross fancy, is actually the lucid statement of an idea as true as any gesture in the picture; it is precisely the relentlessness of its realism in thought as well as in embodiment which frightens people into calling it untrue. The latter two paintings only show that if an artist is realist enough, if he penetrates sufficiently into the actual, he necessarily becomes imaginative; they only reiterate and strengthen Bruegel's right to be considered the supreme realist in painting.

Part of his realism is his refusal to depict what he did not feel. Part of his realism is the robust laughter which is the only solution for the fix in which human beings find themselves. It is the spirit that animated Rabelais in describing the birth of his hero and Shakespeare in creating Falstaff. To come closer home to Bruegel, perhaps, it is the spirit of *Till Eulenspiegel*, whose gross pleasantries were probably relished by the painter along with the rest of his generation.

Bruegel's passion for completeness in his realism abolishes privacy, and the state of affairs brought to pass by this slicing away of all walls is saved only by humor. Humor is the safety-valve for a spirit resolute to probe life to its last refuge—to probe life, but not to break through by main force, as attempted by later realists so-called.

Another element in Bruegel's realism is the objectivity of his work. Van Mander's anecdote, often quoted, shows that Bruegel went among the peasants, not as a professional artist in search of material, but as a participator in their life; and the great pictures themselves strikingly bear this out. This is not to say that Bruegel never worked directly from life, for there are many drawings which could not have been done otherwise—a team of horses resting, soldiers standing in the way, old market-women squatting beside their wares. But when he came to paint the great pictures, Bruegel worked from a memory stocked with the gestures and actions of people who are unconscious of being watched. Bruegel's mind was centered upon their life and he was concerned with technic hardly beyond the point where it would enable him to crowd all their life into his given space and shape. His concentration upon the story he was telling, from the encyclopedic narrative of the early works to the simple and straightforward emotionalism of the *Months,* put him on the crest of a wave of energy

which carried him through many an undertaking
that would have been impossible for a more self-
conscious man. We who see the pictures now are
unconscious of the painter because he was himself lost in his subject; and because of this, also,
we are unconscious of ourselves. "No glance ever
strays across the footlights to the audience,"
wrote Meier-Graefe of Hogarth's scenes. In Bruegel's work there are no actors, no footlights and
no audience. There is only life and participation
in life by painter and by us.

And everywhere in these pictures it is the life
of Bruegel's own time. His predecessors had
clothed religious themes in contemporary dress,
but the outer and the inner remained separate
things; Bruegel, retaining the outer, put into it
its own proper content. He ousted religious stories by contemporary stories. These he painted so
completely that a thorough sociological knowledge of the age might be founded upon or tested
by his pictures. The whole life of the time is set
down by a hand that never falsifies, that swerves
neither to the right of idealization nor to the left
of caricature.

Yet to leave him as a painter of contemporary
manners only would be almost as false to his
greatness as to consider him only as Bruegel the
Droll. For he penetrates below the temporary
appearances of his time to the permanent in human nature. His pictures can be a means of ac-

cess to the life of his age, to be sure; but no lover of them would think of using them in this fashion. The important thing is that they give access to a life that is of more than one age; under the costume of the time exists the same humanity that now wears another dress.

In giving himself over so unreservedly to the impermanent, Bruegel took what was for him the only way to the permanent. This cannot be captured by going out after a vague and unlocalized something called life in general; what is presented to the artist for his use is always life in particular. There is an all-life in the steady and swelling succession of human generations; but the only means of access to that is the now-life. The great artist's major accomplishment lies in revealing the universal through the particular, the permanent through the transitory, the inevitable through the accidental.

This Bruegel does; and how well he does it is to be found by analyzing the thought behind his varied rendering of events and people. Even in his early pictures each creature has his own individuality and yet is part of the crowd, which remains a crowd in spite of all detail; each individual retains his own value of personality and yet is integrated into a collective being. Bruegel's minute accuracy of drawing expresses his love for the individual as such; his great masses of people express his desire to see life largely and as an interwoven whole.

The *Months* sum up his life's endeavor both in the material he had all along been dealing with and in the conceptions between which all along he had been alternating. They are full of motives and incidents taken from his earlier works—the church he drew so often, children at their games, the great stretches of landscape that he loved. But all things are adjusted to one another in a new way; the people are seen neither too large nor too small, but in a perfect relationship to an immensely embracing nature; and each picture is pervaded by an unbroken harmony of mood. This set marks the attainment of final insight into everything that had concerned him; they constitute his acceptance and affirmation of life.

The more Bruegel's work is studied the stronger grows the feeling that almost everything may be attributed to him. To go to Vienna and through that group of fifteen pictures to come into direct contact with his mind across three hundred and fifty years is to be convinced that his is one of the inexhaustible minds of the world. The material brilliancy of the painting is more than matched by the brilliancy of the creative soul behind them. Whether he himself was conscious of all that can now be perceived in his work does not much matter; whether it came there with him aware or unaware, it is enough to make him superbly great. But this much is true: the more his mind is apprehended, the more vast and purposeful it appears.

He was fortunate in finding his means of expression in what was then a popular art; everything about that art was so alive that it drew to itself some of the greatest minds of the time. There existed a tremendous amount of give-and-take between the artist and his age, and this degree of interaction it was which had most to do with endowing both art and artist with vitality; they were fed from sources outside of and larger than themselves. Thus it was that Bruegel attained to so comprehensive an expression of himself and his age together that his work has become one of the permanent things of art.

There are purer painters, but for the purity of their art they pay the price of going without something of importance to a complete life. And even their gain in intensity seems hardly a gain in the face of Bruegel's intensity on all the levels of his completeness. He transposes all life into his pictures in a scale of relative relationship that preserves the values of human life itself. Every other painter lacks something or has something in excess. Bruegel is the most comprehensive and the best balanced, the most energetic and the mellowest. Of all painters he is the greatest realist, and of them all the most humane.

RUBENS

1577 - 1640

For this section on Rubens *we have selected a representative example of the writing of Hippolyte Taine, famous as a philosopher, historian and lecturer. It is an excerpt from a series of talks delivered to his students at the École des Beaux Arts in Paris under the title of "The Philosophy of Art in the Netherlands." This, then represents still another mode of imparting information on art—the formal classroom lecture—as delivered by one of the most famous scholars of his day. Here certainly, it becomes evident that a schoolroom lecture need not be a dry and dusty proposition. Taine has a unique talent for bringing back to life a buried past. As his students listen, the culture which he describes seems to be contemporary and the characters he delineates move freely once more among the living.*

Taine was one of the first lecturers on art and aesthetics to advance the theory that a country's art, whether in the field of painting, sculpture or architecture, reflected the geography, politics and moral temper of the times. He demonstrated the effect of climate on temperament and showed how this temperament reflected itself in the artist's work.

Today Rubens is perhaps the most misunderstood of the world's great artists; for this reason chiefly, we included him in the present group. One may have a fairly accurate notion of current popular taste by listening to the remarks of visitors as they tour the museums and collections. Time and again we note the confusion with which they contemplate this painter's "fat women" posed as nymphs, magdalens or saints. They don't like these naked females; they find them overpowering and repulsive. Since such is the case they dislike the entire picture. This is a very human reaction. As Taine, himself, so aptly expresses it, "Art translates life; the talent and taste of the painter change at the same time and in the same sense as the habits and sentiments of the public." Today, we might better understand Rubens if we could come to consider his pictures with the "habits and sentiments" of his contemporaries. If we succeed in this we may feel with Taine that "no name in the history of art is greater, and there are only three or four as great."

H. J. W.

RUBENS

by

Hippolyte Adolphe Taine

Among the Flemish painters there is one who
seems to efface the rest; indeed no name in the
history of art is greater, and there are only three
or four as great. But Rubens is not an isolated
genius, the number as well as the resemblance
of surrounding talents showing that the efflores-
cence of which he is the most beautiful emana-
tion is the product of his time and people. Before
him there was Adam Van Noort, his master, and
the master of Jordaens. Around him are his contemporaries, educated in other studios, and
whose invention is as spontaneous as his own—
Jordaens, Crayer, and Van Roose. After him
come his pupils—Van den Hoeck, Van Dyck, the
greatest of all, and Van Oost of Bruges. Along-
side of him are the great animal, flower and still-
life painters, and an entire school of famous
engravers. The same sap fructifies all these
branches, the lesser as well as the greater. It is
plain that an art like this is not the effect of one
accidental cause but of a general development.

On the one side it resumes or follows the traditions of Italy, and is seen at a glance to be pagan and Catholic. In fact, there is nothing Christian about it but its name. All mystic or ascetic sentiment is banished; its Madonnas, martyrs and confessors, its Christs and apostles are superb florid bodies restricted to the life of the flesh. Its paradise is an Olympus of well-fed Flemish deities revelling in muscular activity; they are large, vigorous, plump and content, and make a jovial and magnificent display as in a national festival or at a princely entry. The Church, it is true, baptizes this last flower of the old mythology with becoming forms, but it is only baptism, and this is frequently wanting. Apollos, Jupiters, Castors, Pollux and Venus, all the ancient divinities, revive under their veritable names in the palaces of the kings and the great which they decorate. This is owing to religion, here as in Italy, consisting of rites. Rubens goes to mass every morning, and presents a picture in order to obtain indulgences; after which he falls back upon his own poetic feeling for natural life and, in the same style, paints a lusty Magdalen and a plump Siren. Under the Catholic varnish the heart and the intellect, all social ways and observances are pagan. On the other side, this art is truly Flemish; everything issues from and centres on a mother idea which is new and national; it is harmonious, spontaneous and original. From Greece to Florence, from Florence to Venice, from Venice to Antwerp, every step of the passage can be traced. The conception of man and of life goes on decreasing in nobleness and increasing in breadth. Rubens is to Titian what Titian was to Raphael, and Raphael to Phidias. Never did artistic sympathy clasp nature in such an open and universal embrace. There is no respect for historic proprieties; he groups together allegoric with real figures, and cardinals with a naked Mercury. There is no deference to the moral order. He fills the ideal heaven of mythology and of the gospel with coarse or mischievous characters: a Magdalen resembling a nurse, and a Ceres whispering some pleasant gossip in her neighbor's ear. There is no dread of exciting physical sensibility. He pushes the horrible to extremes, athwart all the tortures for the punishment of the flesh and all the contortions of howling agony. There is no fear of offending moral delicacy; his Minerva is a shrew who can fight, his Judith a butcher's wife familiar with blood, and his Paris a jocose expert and a dainty amateur. To translate into words the ideas vociferously proclaimed by his Suzannas and his Magdalens would require the terms of Rabelais. Through him all the animal instincts of human nature appear on the stage. Nothing is wanting but the pure and the noble; the whole of human nature is in his grasp, save the loftiest heights. Hence it is that his creativeness is the vastest we have seen, comprehending as it does all types, Italian cardinals, Roman emperors, contemporary citizens, peasants and cowherds.

For the same reason, in the representation of the body, he comprehended more profoundly than any one the essential characteristics of organic life. He surpasses in this the Venetians, as they surpass the Florentines; he feels still better than they that flesh is a changeable substance in a constant state of renewals. And such, more than any other, is the Flemish body, lymphatic, sanguine and voracious. Hence it is that nobody has depicted its contrasts in stronger relief, nor as visibly shown the decay and bloom of life—at one time the dull flabby corpse, at another the freshness of living carnations, the handsome, blooming and smiling athlete, the soft rosy cheeks and placid candor of a girl whose blood was never quickened by thought. In like manner in the representation of soul and action he appreciated more keenly than any one the essential feature of animal and moral life, that is to say the instantaneous movement which it is the aim of the plastic arts to seize on the wing. In this again he surpasses the Venetians as they surpassed the Florentines. Nobody has endowed figures with such spirit, with a gesture so impulsive, with an impetuosity so abandoned and furious, such a universal commotion and tempest of swollen and writhing muscles in one single effort. His per-

sonages speak; their repose itself is suspended on
the verge of action; we feel what they have just
accomplished and what they are about to do.
The present with them is impregnated with the
past and big with the future. Not only the whole
face but the entire attitude conspires to manifest
the flowing stream of their thought, feeling and
complete being; we hear the inward utterance
of their emotion; we might repeat the words to
which they give expression. The most fleeting
and most subtle shades of sentiment belong to
Rubens. In this respect he is a treasure for novelist and psychologist. He took note of the pass-
ing refinements of moral expression as well as of
the soft volume of sanguine flesh; no one has gone
beyond him in knowledge of the living organism
and of the animal man. Endowed with this sentiment and skill he was capable, in conformity
with the aspirations and needs of his restored
nation, of amplifying the forces he found around
and within himself: on the one hand gigantic
joints, herculean shapes and shoulders, red and
colossal muscles, bearded and truculent heads,
over-nourished bodies teeming with succulence,
the luxurious display of white and rosy flesh; on
the other, the rude instincts which impel human
nature to seek food, drink, strife and pleasure,
the savage fury of the combatant, the enormity
of the big-bellied Silenus, the sensual joviality of
the Faun, the abandonment of that lovely crea-

ture without conscience and "fat with sin," the boldness, the energy, the broad joyousness, the native goodness, the organic serenity of the national type. He heightens these effects again through their composition and the accessories with which he surrounds them—magnificence of lustrous silks, embroidered simarres and golden brocades, groups of naked figures, modern costumes and antique draperies, an inexhaustible accumulation of arms, standards, colonnades, Venetian stairways, temples, canopies, ships, animals, and ever novel and imposing scenery, as if outside of ordinary nature he possessed the key of a thousand times richer nature, whereon his magician's hand could forever draw without the freedom of his imagination ending in confusion, but on the contrary with a jet so vigorous and a prodigality so national that his most complicated productions seem like the irresistible outflow of a surfeited brain. Like an Indian deity at leisure he relieves his fecundity by creating worlds, and from the matchless folds and hues of his tossed simarres to the snowy whites of his flesh, or the pale silkiness of his blonde tresses, there is no tone in any of his canvases which does not appear there purposely to afford him delight.

There is only one Rubens in Flanders, as there is only one Shakespeare in England. Great as the others are, they are deficient in some one element of his genius.

REMBRANDT

1606 - 1669

In his highly imaginative *pen portrait of the Dutch painter Rembrandt van Rijn, Mr. van Loon employs an interesting literary device to recreate for us the life and times of the artist. He assumes the rôle of a "great-grandson, nine times removed, of one Joannis van Loon, a Dutch physician who was a contemporary and friend of Rembrandt." His ancestor is supposed to have written down these personal recollections of the greatest of his fellow citizens.*

Although there have been countless volumes written on the subject of Rembrandt's art we know of few which so completely recreate the period and the atmosphere in which he worked, and none which give so penetrating a glance into the mind and the heart of this creative genius.

We have selected a chapter deep in the book where the physician visits Rembrandt who suddenly "becomes talkative" and favors the doctor "with a few of his views upon art." It is interesting to note how the period described parallels our own and how little the relationship between artist and public has changed.

Hendrik Willem van Loon was born in Rotterdam, Holland in 1882. He came to this country as a young man and achieved a distinguished success in a very short time. The Story of Mankind, The Story of the Bible, *and* Van Loon's Geography *were widely read in this country as well as in translations all over the world.*

I recall a conversation with Van Loon shortly after the publication of his Life and Times of Rembrandt van Rijn. *This astonishing man, capable of such prodigious feats of research, compilation and imaginative writing complained that not enough copies of his beloved* Rembrandt *were being sold. Of all the books he had completed to 1931, this was the one which taxed his skill and energy the most. He considered it by far his best work and poured into its making all his heart and spirit.*

Little did Van Loon realize that his book was ultimately to sell more copies than any work on Rembrandt in English or any other language. If the Dutch painter needed anything more than his etchings and canvases to make him immortal, this literary achievement of his spiritual descendant would certainly have served the purpose.

H. J. W.

REMBRANDT

by

Hendrik Willem van Loon

Notwithstanding the war, which continued with uneven success, there was a good deal of money abroad at that time. Thousands of people were losing all they had; but a few hundred, who had been shrewd enough to speculate in grain and wood and gun-powder and all the other supplies of which the fleet was in such great need, made vast sums of money. Not knowing what to do with their newly found riches, they were buying luxuries right and left.

One day pictures would be all the rage. The next day it would be china. The little Japanese cups that had sold for three florins apiece had gone up to three thousand. The china craze switched over to pearls, and when all the wives of all the profiteers had been provided with earrings as large as carrots, pearls became vulgar almost over night and the Nuremberg watchmakers reaped a fortune with queer and extraordinary timepieces that showed not only the minutes but also the seconds and that played a little tune when the hour was struck, just like the bells of the new town hall.

As they had heard that there lived a painter in the Jewish quarter whose house was a museum of everything that one could possibly hope to collect, a good many of them found their way to the Breestraat.

In the beginning, Rembrandt felt rather flattered, and thought that this meant a renewed interest in his own work. But very soon he discovered that those noisy visitors with their even more noisy wives did not care in the least for his own art—very often were ignorant of his name—called him Ronnebrandt or Remscheidt—patronized him in most outrageous fashion—gave Titus sweetmeats and patted his head and said he was a nice little Jewish boy and then asked the master how much he would take for an enameled Turkish sword or a piece of ivory carving from the Indies. Then he would grow angry at such an indignity (for he well knew the value of his own work) and instead of making these miserable war profiteers pay an outrageous sum for some article which he himself had bought in a moment of weakness and for which his visitors were willing to pay ten times the original price, he would show them the door in a most abrupt fashion (he still could speak the vernacular of the Weddesteeg in Leyden with great fluency) and then these amazing guests would depart and would spread it among all their friends that this man Rompot, that so-called artist, who gave himself such airs, was an ill-natured ruffian and that one ought to give him a wide berth and have nothing to do with him.

Until the rumor had gone all over town that the painter was a sullen and crabbed barbarian—a morose and splenetic fellow—whose swinish ill-temper had turned him into an involuntary recluse, shunned by all his neighbors for his violence and irascibility.

Nothing could have been less true than that. Rembrandt was of this earth earthy. He was fashioned out of the common clay of our land and our land, lest we forget, lies fifteen feet below sea-level. But he had one enormous advantage over the majority of his neighbors. Like most other artists he had a purpose in life and he was too busy with his own problems to enjoy that leisure which is the breeding ground of gossip and spite.

I sometimes hinted at books as a substitute for the infinitely more expensive objects of art with which he filled his room.

"You have been telling me to be careful," he said. "Everybody I ever knew has been telling me to be careful. You are a man of tact (that is why I like you) and rather than tell me outright not to buy pictures and helmets and all those things in this room and in the others" (he made a gesture that meant to include the whole house) "you have encouraged me to buy books—and read.

"You remind me of those people who have been coming to me ever since I was fourteen years old and had smeared some paint (very badly I am afraid) on a couple of pieces of canvas. 'My dear boy,' they used to say, 'this is all very nice and very pretty but it will never lead to anything. You can't learn your trade here. We in the North are all of us barbarians when it comes to the arts. Italy, the South, that is the country for you.'

"I used to make them very angry with my attitude. 'Painting,' I used to say, 'is nothing but seeing. You see something that impresses you and then you paint it, or if you have a gift for something else, then you draw it or hack it out of a piece of marble, as the Greeks used to do, or you make a tune out of it and play it on the organ.'

"And then I would add that it did not depend so much upon what you saw as how you saw it and that a good artist could get more inspiration out of a dead bullock hanging from a ladder in some mean village butcher-shop, than a bad one out of half a dozen beautiful churches in the village where Raphael himself was born.

"All this sounded like terrible heresies to the good people among whom I grew up. All I meant was that the Italians living in Italy should get their emotion (the word inspiration is good enough for theologians and for amateur artists) from Italian subjects, but that we people living in Holland should get our emotions from the subjects with which we were familiar in our own country and not from something a thousand miles away.

"So, when I was very young I had thought that painting was merely a matter of seeing, of feeling, of sensing some particular object or idea and translating. One day I was working in my father's mill and something happened to me. I don't mean that I was painting in my father's mill. In those early days I was not encouraged very much to become an artist. My people were simple folk and very pious. They had the usual prejudice against the arts and especially against the artists. When one mentioned the word painter, they thought of Babylon and Sodom at once, and when I first told them that I wanted to be a great painter, like Lucas van Leyden, who was the first man whose works I had ever seen, they shook their heads and said 'No,' they wanted me to be a good Christian and get ahead in the world.

"I seemed to have a fairly good brain—I was much cleverer than my brothers. One of them could succeed father in the mill and the others would be taught a trade that they might spend their days as God-fearing members in good standing of some honorable guild of artisans. But as for me I was to go to the university and get a degree so that my parents could say, 'Our son, the Doctor of Laws,' and have something to console themselves for the hard labor which had been their share all during the time they were bringing us up.

"That plan never came to anything. I actually went to the university but I was a dreadful failure as a student. I never went to a single lecture. I wrote my name in a big book and got a piece of paper informing me most solemnly that Rembrandus Hermanius Leydensis or some such thing was now, at the age of fourteen, if you please, a duly enrolled stud-litt—whatever that meant—in the glorious university of Leyden, and entitled to all the rights and privileges connected with this distinguished rank.

"But it was no use, I never went near a professor or a book (I cared as little about books then as I do now) and instead I went to Jaap Swanenburch, who was a famous man in our town—he was one of those who had learned their trade in Italy—he had done the job so thoroughly, he even came home with an Italian wife who used to throw plates and knives at him every time we had a pretty model, to the great joy and delectation of his pupils—and when Swanenburch came to the Weddesteeg one day and told my parents that I had it in me to become a most successful and fashionable portrait painter, but

would they please pay my tuition, they forgave
me for having played hookey from my scholarly
duties and as Swanenburch's charges were less
than the tuition fee of the university, they de-
cided that they might as well let me stay where
I was and work out my own salvation according
to the best of my own abilities.

"But before that time, I could only draw when
no one was looking my way and every afternoon
after school time, my brother Cornelis and I used
to go to the mill on the wall and help father with
his work. Have you ever been in a mill? You have.
Ever been in a mill on a bright, sun-shiny sort of a
day? Well, then you have missed something. For
the wings do curious things to the interior on a
day like that. There was a brisk eastern wind
blowing outside and the wings went past the
window, g'chuck—g'chuck—g'chuck, just a sort
of guttural sound like the snapping of a musket
and then the sudden swish of those enormous
wooden arms, cleaving the air. And every time
one of those wings passed by one of the windows,
the light was cut off for perhaps a hundredth
part of a second—just a flash—too short to measure by the clock—but visible, just the same—very
visible indeed, for every time it happened, the
room became pitch dark.

"Now you may remember that when we were
young, the country was suffering from a plague
of rats. There were people who did nothing all

their lives long except catch rats—professional rat-catchers. They were usually old soldiers and very dirty and very picturesque and I have drawn them quite a lot, for they were interesting-looking scoundrels.

"That morning one of them had been at work in our mill. The rat-catcher would not be back before evening and one enormous wire cage full of rats was hanging by a strong chain from a rafter of the mill. Through the scurrying and pattering of all these excited little bodies, with their bright beady eyes and their long, disgusting tails, the cage was slowly beginning to swing from left to right and it was making a curious shadow upon the wall. And all the time, the wings of the mill kept swishing past the window and every time they swished past, the room would be pitch dark and then for just one, two, three seconds, it would be filled once more with brilliant sunlight.

"But I had seen that sort of thing hundreds of times before and it had never struck me as anything very remarkable. And then suddenly—it really came to me just like the revelation that came to Saul—I noticed that the cage was not merely hanging in the light or in the air, as I had always taken for granted, but that it was an object surrounded by a whole lot of different sorts of air—all of which were of a different texture. In the beginning it was not at all clear to me and I can't expect to tell you what I mean in two words, but you know of course that there are a number of colors, like yellow and blue and red and combinations of colors and we painters are supposed to know all about those colors and their combinations and that is how we paint our pictures. We tell stories in daubs of color, just as others tell stories in lines or with the help of words or notes. At least, that is what I had always taken for granted and I had done my best to learn how to use those colors.

"But that morning in the mill, there weren't any colors, at least, none of the colors with which I had been familiar from my earliest childhood, when some one gave me my first box of paints. The light in front of that rat cage was different from the light behind it, which was different again from the light on the left of it and all these different sorts of light did not remain the same, but changed every moment. Of course, when I say 'light' I mean air and when I say air, I mean light. What I really mean is the space which fills all our rooms and all our houses and the whole world—the stuff we breathe, and through which the birds fly. And then the idea suddenly struck me (and that was the moment when I turned from Saul to Paul) does all this space—this air— really have a color in our sense of the word and is it possible to translate that color into terms of paint?

"Let me show you" (here he picked up a pewter mug that was standing on the table)—"let me show you. You see that mug. It is about three feet away from you. And now" (moving it towards himself) "it is only two feet away. Suppose I want to paint this. I can get the illusion of distance by applying the rules of perspective which Master Dürer of Nuremberg laid down in that little book of his. That would be enough when I use a pencil or pen and ink. But when I use color, I ought to be able to create that impression of distance in some other way—in the way nature does it, or rather, in the way I suspect that nature does it. For I have now spent the greater part of every day during the last forty years—Sundays included, to the horror of my good parents—trying to solve the problem and I know just as little about it to-day as I did when I first began.

"But from that moment on, from the moment I saw those excited rats in their wire cage, hanging from the rafter of my father's mill, until to-day I have been convinced that every object in the world is surrounded by a substance (call it light or air or space or whatever you like) which somehow or other it must be possible to express in the terms of light and shade and half a dozen primary colors.

"Sometimes I even think that at least in a few of my pictures I have solved that problem pretty well. But I confess that I have been working backwards, painting the picture first and trying to discover afterwards why I had done what I had done. People, always looking for the outlandish and the unusual, whisper that I have a secret. Secret fiddlesticks! I am a mathematician who works in vegetable matter and who started out with a formula and who is now trying to prove that it works and is correct.

"I probably would have been more of a success in my work if I had not been told by my father to work in his mill on that particular morning. Now I waste half of my time or more on a problem that no one has ever solved before me— that no one, as far as I can find out, has even thought of. Rubens is a great man, but he does not even suspect that there is such a thing as I have been trying to put into paint for the last thirty years. Hals comes much nearer to it. That man Brouwer (you scolded me because I bought so many of his pictures) has done marvels in that field. They tell me there is a man in Spain, working for the King (his name is Velásquez, or Velázquez, I don't quite know) who seems to be working on that basis. I have never seen any of his paintings and it is always difficult to imagine what a picture looks like merely from hearing some one else describe it.

"Of course, the public has no notion of what I am trying to do. They sneer, 'He does not paint things the way we ourselves see them.'

"Heaven forbid them that I should ever see

things the way they do! They may (and very likely they will) let me starve, but they can't rob me of the conviction that I am right and that they are wrong. Any one can learn to paint the things that are there. But to paint the things that one merely suspects to be there while one can't possibly prove that they are there—that, my good Doctor, that is the sort of task that makes life interesting. And that is the sort of thing that makes other people be afraid of me"

We went to the back room. Titus was fast asleep in one of the two beds built in the wall. Hendrickje went to get the wine and the spices that were necessary for our hot drink. The kettle was standing on the floor in front of the fire. She leaned over to pick it up just as I looked her way. And suddenly my professional eye registered an unmistakable professional fact. She was pregnant and in her seventh or eighth month.

That too was a problem in space but one which Rembrandt seemed to have overlooked.

RIGHT: PL. 42

EL GRECO

SELF-PORTRAIT

EL GRECO

PL. 43

View of Toledo

EL GRECO   PL. 44

VIEW OF TOLEDO
[DETAIL]

EL GRECO

PL. 45

VIRGIN WITH SAINTS

[DETAIL]

EL GRECO   PL. 46

Virgin with Saints
[detail]

EL GRECO

CARDINAL NINO DE GUEVARA

EL GRECO   PL. 48

St. Jerome

EL GRECO   PL. 49

PIETA

RIGHT: PL. 50

DIEGO VELASQUEZ

SELF-PORTRAIT

VELASQUEZ   PL. 51

Infanta Margarita

VELASQUEZ   PL. 52

DON BALTHASAR ON HORSEBACK

VELASQUEZ   PL. 53

Court Dwarf

VELASQUEZ   PL. 54

PORTRAIT OF A YOUNG MAN

VELASQUEZ

LOS BORRACHOS

VELASQUEZ

VENUS AND CUPID

VELASQUEZ   PL. 57

The Infanta

EL GRECO

1548? - 1625

THE FOLLOWING REFERENCES TO EL GRECO *and
the extraordinary evaluation of his art, appear in
the pages of Mr. Somerset Maugham's novel, Of
Human Bondage. This selection offers brilliant
proof that the discussion of art and artists need
not be confined to the textbook or to ponderous
volumes on aesthetics or art history. It is certainly appropriate that such discussions take
place in the home as well as the classroom and
that ordinary folk as well as scholars dare talk in
lively terms about pictures or their makers.*

*The following scene is fiction, and the charac-
ters are the product of Mr. Maugham's unique
skill as a novelist. In this instance, the author
has his character Athelny discuss the painter El
Greco in a manner which reveals Maugham's
keen understanding. Though now acknowledged
one of the great masters, El Greco was hardly
known to critics or public 50 years ago. The
French art critic Arsène Alexandre wrote in a letter to Maurice Barrès:*

"At this time (1890) I had ample proof, at To-

ledo itself, of the oblivion and disdain to which the Spaniards had condemned poor Theotoco-poulos ... I had the greatest difficulty in finding someone who could tell me in which church was to be found the admirable 'Burial of Count Orgaz' and once this was determined it was more difficult yet to get someone to open the little church of Santo-Tomé, for it had been continuously locked up!"

El Greco, a Greek, was born on the island of Crete, was formed in the studio of the great Venetian painter Tintoretto and left his finest pictures on the walls of an obscure church in Toledo, Spain. There is a painting by El Greco in the Louvre, a Crucifixion which I think is the most inspiring representation of its kind in the whole of art history. Without El Greco's background of training and inheritance I do not think it could have been painted. It is derived from no masters and produced no copies. Against a sky of storm and tempest is silhouetted the attenuated, athletic figure of a Christ suited by his physique and his noble serenity to be the hero of the Christian Story. It is inconceivable that the maker of such a picture could so long languish in a limbo of forgotten masters. It is a tribute to modern artists and writers on art that El Greco has finally the appreciation he deserves.

H. J. W.

EL GRECO

by

W. Somerset Maugham

Athelny got up from his chair, walked over
to the Spanish cabinet, let down the front with
its great gilt hinges and gorgeous lock, and displayed a series of little drawers. He took out a
bundle of photographs.

"Do you know El Greco?" he asked.

"Oh, I remember one of the men in Paris was
awfully impressed by him."

"El Greco was the painter of Toledo. Betty
couldn't find the photograph I wanted to show
you. It's a picture that El Greco painted of the
city he loved, and it's truer than any photograph.
Come and sit at the table."

Philip dragged his chair forward, and Athelny
set the photograph before him. He looked at it
curiously, for a long time, in silence. He stretched
out his hand for other photographs, and Athelny
passed them to him. He had never before seen
the work of that enigmatic master; and at the
first glance he was bothered by the arbitrary
drawing: the figures were extraordinarily elon-
gated; the heads were very small; the attitudes

were extravagant. This was not realism, and yet, and yet even in the photographs you had the impression of a troubling reality. Athelny was describing eagerly, with vivid phrases, but Philip only heard vaguely what he said. He was puzzled. He was curiously moved. These pictures seemed to offer some meaning to him, but he did not know what the meaning was. There were portraits of men with large, melancholy eyes which seemed to say you knew not what; there were long monks in the Franciscan habit or in the Dominican, with distraught faces, making gestures whose sense escaped you; there was an Assumption of the Virgin; there was a Crucifixion in which the painter by some magic of feeling had been able to suggest that the flesh of Christ's dead body was not human flesh only but divine; and there was an Ascension in which the Saviour seemed to surge up towards the empyrean and yet to stand upon the air as steadily as though it were solid ground: the uplifted arms of the Apostles, the sweep of their draperies, their ecstatic gestures, gave an impression of exultation and of holy joy. The background of nearly all was the sky by night, the dark night of the soul, with wild clouds swept by strange winds of hell and lit luridly by an uneasy moon.

"I've seen that sky in Toledo over and over again," said Athelny. "I have an idea that when first El Greco came to the city it was by such a night, and it made so vehement an impression upon him that he could never get away from it."

Philip remembered how Clutton had been affected by this strange master, whose work he now saw for the first time. He thought that Clutton was the most interesting of all the people he had known in Paris. His sardonic manner, his hostile aloofness, had made it difficult to know him; but it seemed to Philip, looking back, that there had been in him a tragic force, which sought vainly to express itself in painting. He was a man of unusual character, mystical after the fashion of a time that had no leaning to mysticism, who was impatient with life because he found himself unable to say the things which the obscure impulses of his heart suggested. His intellect was not fashioned to the uses of the spirit. It was not surprising that he felt a deep sympathy with the Greek who had devised a new technique to express the yearnings of his soul. Philip looked again at the series of portraits of Spanish gentlemen, with ruffles and pointed beards, their faces pale against the sober black of their clothes and the darkness of the background. El Greco was the painter of the soul; and these gentlemen, wan and wasted, not by exhaustion but by restraint, with their tortured minds, seem to walk unaware of the beauty of the world; for their eyes look only in their hearts, and they are dazzled by the glory of the unseen.

No painter has shown more pitilessly that the world is but a place of passage. The souls of the men he painted speak their strange longings through their eyes: their senses are miraculously acute, not for sounds and odours and colour, but for the very subtle sensations of the soul. The noble walks with the monkish heart within him, and his eyes see things which saints in their cells see too, and he is unastounded. His lips are not lips that smile.

Philip, silent still, returned to the photograph of Toledo, which seemed to him the most arresting picture of them all. He could not take his eyes off it. He felt strangely that he was on the threshold of some new discovery in life. He was tremulous with a sense of adventure. He thought for an instant of the love that had consumed him: love seemed very trivial beside the excitement which now leaped in his heart. The picture he looked at was a long one, with houses crowded upon a hill; in one corner a boy was holding a large map of the town; in another was a classical figure representing the river Tagus; and in the sky was the Virgin surrounded by angels. It was a landscape alien to all Philip's notions, for he had lived in circles that worshipped exact realism; and yet here again, strangely to himself, he felt a reality greater than any achieved by the masters in whose steps humbly he had sought to walk. He heard Athelny say that the representation was so precise that when the citizens of Toledo came to look at the picture they recognised their houses. The painter had painted exactly what he saw, but he had seen with the eyes of the spirit. There was something unearthly in that city of pale gray. It was a city of the soul seen by a wan light that was neither that of night nor day. It stood on a green hill, but of a green not of this world, and it was surrounded by massive walls and bastions to be stormed by no machines or engines of man's invention, but by prayer and fasting, by contrite sighs and by mortifications of the flesh. It was a stronghold of God. Those gray houses were made of no stone known to masons, there was something terrifying in their aspect, and you did not know what men might live in them. You might walk through the streets and be unamazed to find them all deserted, and yet not empty; for you felt a presence invisible and yet manifest to every inner sense. It was a mystical city in which the imagination faltered like one who steps out of the light into darkness; the soul walked naked to and fro, knowing the unknowable, and conscious strangely of experience, intimate but inexpressible, of the absolute. And without surprise, in that blue sky, real with a reality that not the eye but the soul confesses, with its rack of light clouds driven by strange breezes, like the cries and the sighs of lost souls, you saw the Blessed Virgin with a gown of red and a cloak of blue, surrounded by winged angels. Philip felt that the inhabitants of that city would have seen the apparition without astonishment, reverent and thankful, and have gone their ways.

Athelny spoke of the mystical writers of Spain, of Teresa de Avila, San Juan de la Cruz, Fray Diego de Leon; in all of them was that passion for the unseen which Philip felt in the pictures of El Greco: they seemed to have the power to touch the incorporeal and see the invisible. They were proud, for they were masters of the world. Life was passionate and manifold, and because it offered so much they felt a restless yearning for something more; because they were human they were unsatisfied; and they threw this eager vitality of theirs into a vehement striving after the ineffable. Athelny was not displeased to find someone to whom he could read the translations with which for some time he had amused his leisure; and in his fine, vibrating voice he recited the canticle of the Soul and Christ her lover, the lovely poem which begins with the words *en una noche oscura,* and the *noche serena* of Fray Luis de Leon. He had translated them quite simply, not without skill, and he had found words which at all events suggested the rough-hewn grandeur of the original. The pictures of El Greco explained them, and they explained the pictures.

VELASQUEZ

1599 - 1660

IN THOMAS CRAVEN, *we have perhaps the most talked-of writer on art in our time. His* Men of Art *was the first book of its kind to be read cover to cover by an avid public long waiting for someone to address them squarely in just such a fashion. In Mr. Craven's pages artists come alive. They are no longer moldy characters out of textbooks and encyclopedias, but sentient humans with lusts and ambitions, passions and hates. We begin to understand better the times which produced them. Craven does for history what he does for the artist, and gives dates and placenames a new meaning. With the artist thus silhouetted against the background of his own age we see him reacting to wars, plagues, persecutions and prosperity. We see him in his personal environment, the quiet studio, the bourgeois home. How much easier it is to understand why he paints as he does. It is no wonder that Mr. Craven has won more converts to the cause of art than any writer of our day.*

In his opinions of art and artists Thomas Cra-

ven never sits a fence. He is plainly on one side or the other. He says what he thinks and what he thinks often runs counter to the current trend. I think he is a man to welcome an argument. But he would respect the antagonist who stated his case well. If only there were more such provocative talk and writing about art!

In the painting of Diego Velasquez we have a startling example of the slight importance of subject matter; if the artist brings to the subject his own poetic vision he can transmute dross into gold. When Velasquez painted portraits of the members of the Spanish court, the royal personalities themselves, the buffoons and dwarfs, he had as unprepossessing a group of models as ever sat for an artist. He made of these portraits things of wonder and the "Monstrous Girl" of the Prado, "Mariana of Austria" or the "Count Baltasar" all stand in their frames "as if alive." Here we have the art of portraiture brought to its finest flowering. These canvases alone are enough to rank Velasquez with the greatest of the painters.

H. J. W.

VELASQUEZ

by

Thomas Craven

THE DESCENT from El Greco's far-flung visions into the matter-of-fact world of Velasquez is sudden and refreshing. It affords a solid exhilaration such as we should experience in turning from the soul-troubles of Dostoievsky to the pellucid objectivity of Ernest Hemingway's novels. There are no soul-troubles in Velasquez, no troubles indeed of any sort: the overwhelming religious tragedy of Spain, the decaying glory of the Empire; rebellion in Holland and Portugal; the sickening society of the Hapsburgs—none of these caused him a moment of uneasiness. Cooped up in the King's closet; painting, at the King's pleasure, the abortions of the court; compelled to bow to the criticisms of His Majesty, himself a dabbler in paint, he lost neither his distinction nor his independence, never shirked his job, never complained of the monotony of his servitude. If he was bored or lonely, if he was light-hearted or oppressed by his confinement, he kept his feelings buried within himself. His work is abnormally free from passions and philosophies; he is the most reserved, the most disinterested of men—and for those to whom art is the scientific statement of the facts of the visible world, the faultless painter.

Velasquez was a Portuguese aristocrat born in Sevilla in 1599. His father, desiring him to enter one of the learned professions, had him carefully educated, so an old Sevillian informs us; but his education could not have been very extensive, for he determined at an early age to become a painter, and having proved his skill, was apprenticed in his thirteenth year to Herrera, an artist of some prominence in southern Spain. The association did not prosper: Herrera was half-mad and given to spells of inexcusable cruelty, and his pupil soon left him for the more amiable and scholarly Pacheco in whose house he lived for five years. Pacheco was not much of a painter, but he was a man of superior tastes, of estimable ambitions, and a charming companion. Furthermore, he had a daughter. He was strong for Raphael, but Velasquez did not take to Raphael, nor to any of the Florentines, and while the master proclaimed the sublimity of classic art, the young hidalgo painted Andalusian peasants—and made love to Juana. At nineteen, fully grown and the best painter in the South, and in all Spain save for the Cretan at Toledo, he married the girl, "moved thereto," Pacheco says, "by her virtue, beauty and good qualities and his trust in his own natural genius."

He was spared the privations, the long immaturity, and the dark introspections which so many painters have had to suffer. Never was an artist more contented with his environment, or less open to new experiences. His world began and ended at the court of King Philip. His travels in Italy had no effect on him unless it were in the modification of his color, but even that, I am inclined to believe, came to him as it came to the modern Impressionists, from his marvellously acute perception of atmospheric values.

The Venetians alone called forth his admiration, and in his *Memoria De Las Pinturas,* a book unknown to all his biographers, he records, in Spanish as clear and pure as the language of his brush, his praise of Tintoretto and Veronese. His notes on Tintoretto's *Washing of the Feet,* might well be a description of one of his own canvases, and show us exactly what he expected of the art of painting. "It is hard to believe," he writes, "that one is looking at a painting. Such is the truth of color, such the exactness of perspective, that one might think to go in and walk on the pavement, tessellated with stones of divers colors, which, diminishing in size, make the room seem larger, and lead one to believe that there is atmosphere between the figures. The tables, seats—and a dog which is worked in—are truth, not paint. . . . Once for all, any picture placed beside it looks like something expressed in terms of color, and this, therefore, seems all the truer."

Despite the apparent simplicity of Velasquez's point of view, it is not a simple matter to explain the conjunction of his impassive personality with the facts of life, and harder still is it to describe the peculiar satisfaction derived from his paintings. He knew very little about the organic structure of the human body, and was as ignorant of the universal aspects of art as was his wife, Juana. His is the science of externals, the logic of light and shade. He approached his subjects in what might be termed the spirit of scientific purity, examining them in the atmosphere of his studio with truly spectroscopical precision. He is responsible for the theory inscribed defiantly on the red banners of Modernism, namely, that *it is not what one paints but how*. His attitude towards his subjects, borrowed by the French, became the staple of the Impressionists and was pithily expressed in a remark commonly fathered upon Cézanne: the artist should have as much respect for a cheese or a cabbage as for a human head.

The royal family was not more agreeable to his brush than the indentured morons of the court. Every day, when the ungainly King entered his studio, a new problem in the visual aspects of matter presented itself. That was all. The King was treated as still-life. Time and again he painted him, but we know no more of him in the last pictures than in the first, and no more of the artist, save that his eye grew more searching, his handling of pigment more dextrous, his tones more silvery and enchanting. He painted the King's face in precisely the same spirit as his modern kinsman Monet painted haystacks—the same old stacks twenty times over to prove that the atmosphere is colored and the color varies with the march of the sun.

It is difficult to discuss this man in any but a technical language, difficult because his fame and influence, for the most part, rest upon his ability to handle paint. Technically, he is generally acknowledged to be the greatest of painters, although a good case might be made for Vermeer. But it does not matter. Let us concede his preëminence, not forgetting, however, that by technique we mean craftsmanship and not the inevitable form evolved by every artist who has anything to say. Velasquez's eye was practically unerring; his hand obedient to his eye; his touch inexpressibly sensitive.

Connoisseurs, seduced by his "beautiful painting," praise his charms in the cadences of a lover doting on a fresh mistress. They smack their lips over the rose and grey stuff, extol the purity of tones blended with the lightness of water-color, grow eloquent over the caressing softness of brush-strokes that twist a little blob of paint into a lip or a bit of lace, talk of the "muted melodies" of his color, and shout in adoration of his infinite tact when he drops a touch of color into a shadow—the final fleck to define the top of the nose. All of which is fine and rare and delightful to the eye.

In analyzing Velasquez's straightforward approach to life, I have, perhaps, over-emphasized his literalness. His heads are not the emotionally flat images recorded by the camera; his harmonies do not exist ready-made in nature. What he gives us is an intensified version of the visible world. I have spoken of the peculiar satisfaction of his paintings, a satisfaction, as we now see, deriving from his perfectly normal point of view. Here is a man unencumbered by a heavy burden of ideals and philosophies; here is an artist who gives us, not the dignity of man, but the dignity of matter.

In Velasquez this is refreshing; of his followers we cannot say as much. After him there is no further need for architectural painting; he made it easy for non-thinking artists to usurp the field; he directed attention to the dignity of material things by suppressing the spiritual, and his disciples, completing the ruin of the classical edifice, have taken the mind out of painting altogether and reduced it to the level of barren processes.

RIGHT: PL. 58

JAN VERMEER OF DELFT

THE ARTIST'S STUDIO

VERMEER   PL. 59

THE LACE MAKER

VERMEER PL. 60

YOUNG WOMAN WITH A WATER JUG

VERMEER   PL. 61

The Lace Maker

VERMEER

The Milkmaid

VERMEER   PL. 63

A Woman Weighing Gold

VERMEER   PL. 64

LITTLE STREET IN DELFT

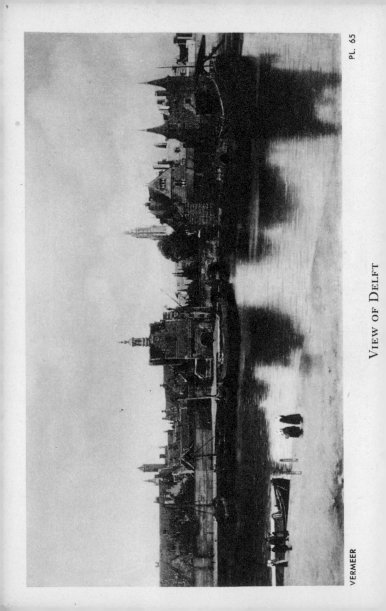

VERMEER

VIEW OF DELFT

VERMEER

1632 - 1675

It is difficult *to write with great emotion
about the art or personality of Jan Vermeer,
painter of Delft. There are more robust and
colorful characters who painted pictures, and
there are countless portraits, landscapes and
scenes of action more apt to quicken the pulse
of the observer. But when it comes to representing through the magic of brush strokes the every-
day world in which we live—little streets or river
banks, rooms with treasured personal belongings,
rugs and porcelain vases, musical instruments
and pictured tapestries—he had no equal. There
is a peculiarly static quality in the painting of
Vermeer which lends an added virtue. It is as
though only the pleasant and tranquil moments
of man's experience were deemed worthy of record. There is dignified enjoyment of life with
nothing lusty or boisterous depicted. There are
comparatively few religious scenes painted by
this master but there is more of goodness and
inward peace suggested in his pictures than in
most religious pictures. The women in his paint-*

ings are certainly less fleshly than the saints of Rubens and often not so sensual as Raphael's famed Madonnas.

It may be said that in the pictures of Vermeer we find ennobled the home life of good and righteous people. He left to some of his contemporaries the realistic depiction of the tavern life with its drunken play and to others the rich legends of fable, with lush nymphs and fauns. Vermeer has brought poetry to the subject of a "Young Girl at a Spinet," a "Lady Writing," or the simple view of a room with "A Girl Asleep."

The piece which follows is from the first chapter of Vermeer by Philip L. Hale. Here is an example of sound scholarship, with a text written in the quiet mood of Vermeer's paintings. Mr. Hale was himself a painter, a teacher and a lecturer. He was born in Boston, Massachusetts in 1865, of lineage stemming back to Nathan Hale, the American patriot. Since we have sought in this volume to achieve range and variety in styles of writing, it should be interesting for the reader to contrast the following chapter by Philip Hale, with Taine's treatment of Rubens.

Vermeer is one of the few painters of whom we have no authenticated self-portrait. We have therefore, included in our selection of illustrations the picture known as "A Painter's Studio" and sometimes called "Portrait of the Artist."

H. J. W.

VERMEER

by

Philip L. Hale

THE BEST MEN in art are found by a process of elimination. It may be a challenging statement to call Jan Vermeer of Delft the greatest painter who has ever lived. Yet in sheer downright painting, he was in most respects the leader of all. There were giants, of course, such as Velasquez, Rubens and Rembrandt, who did very wonderful things, but none of these ever conceived of arriving at tone by an exquisitely just relation of colour values—the essence of contemporary painting that is really good.

Various qualities in Vermeer's work are those for which the best painters of our day strive: his design, his colour values, his edges, his way of using the square touch, his occasionally *pointillé* touch, all of which are qualities that one seldom observes in other old masters. We of today particularly admire Vermeer because he has attacked what seem to us significant problems or motives, and has solved them, on the whole, as we like to see them solved. And with this he has been able to retain something of the serenity, poise and finish that we regard as peculiarly the property of the old masters. Our present-day work is often petulant; that of the old masters was generally serene.

True it is, as will appear in the discussion to follow, that Vermeer was not always wholly successful. Nobody ever has been, and doubtless no one ever will be. It is silly to ascribe to one's hero all the virtues; it is enough to point out the qualities which he possesses.

By and large, Vermeer has more great painting qualities and fewer defects than any other painter of any time or place. He was born in 1632 and died at the age of forty-three in 1675; and it is when one compares him with other great artists of his own day and land that his superiority is most manifest. Terborch, by comparison with Vermeer, appears sleazy and mannered; de Hooch looks hot and stodgy; even Metsu, perhaps the most accomplished technician of them all, seems rather artificial and by no means alert to colour values. Each of these men, of course, had extraordinary qualities. But Vermeer combined within himself most of their good qualities and avoided many of their defects.

His manner of seeing is the basic excellence of Vermeer's art—the thing that sets it apart from the work of other men. Where others had a genius for drawing or for colouration, he had a genius for vision. One arrives, while studying his work carefully, at a feeling that he looked at things harder than others have looked at them. Many painters acquire a manner of making things, a *parti-pris,* which impels them to distort nature to suit their book. Vermeer, too, had his manner of workmanship, but after he had laid his picture in, and indeed carried it quite far, he seems to have sat back and looked at what was before him again and again to see if there was anything he could do to his picture to make it portray more closely the real aspect of nature —*la vraie vérité,* as Gustave Courbet liked to call it. His almost perfect rendering was the outcome of perfect understanding.

Vermeer's art has the quality of cool, well-planned rightness to the full. He holds, as it were, a silver mirror up to nature, but he tells no merely pleasant tale as he holds it. His work is as intensely personal as any that was ever done, but it offers a personality disengaged from self-consciousness during the making process.

His name is not surrounded by the kind of fame for which a more accurate word is notoriety. He was no playboy of the boulevards, he did not run away with some rival painter's wife, he did not do eccentric things of the kind for which, again, the better term is egocentric. On the contrary, so little was known of him for about two hundred and fifty years that the impression became fixed that almost nothing at all was known about him. Following the lead of his "rediscoverer," M. Théophile Thoré, who called him "the Sphinx of Delft," those members of the general public who knew anything about him at all—even so much as his name—thought of him as a man of mystery. They came almost to doubt his very existence and to wonder how pictures painted so entrancingly could be the work of a man so little known and so completely without any background of alluring anecdote. Indeed, as we shall see, many of his pictures themselves were for years attributed to other painters, some through ignorance, some through deliberate fraud, because they would sell better if they bore some other name than his—some name that was at the moment better known.

It may truly be said that the real romance of Vermeer is the extraordinary story of how he sank into oblivion, slumbered for centuries and then came again out of his deep obscurity into the light of fame. For, as we shall see, he was by no means an unimportant figure in his own day. Modern research has established the fact that he attained the status of master painter in the Guild of St. Luke at Delft when he was barely twenty-one, the son of parents who came from families on the whole of fairly substantial means; that he was mentioned in a poem written when he was scarcely twenty-two in a way which indicates how highly he was considered as a young man of promise; that he had already married at twenty the daughter of a woman who clearly regarded him as a good and dependable son-in-law throughout his comparatively short life; that he was, during at least four different years, one of the six Syndics of the Guild and for two of those years their chairman or president; that he was especially visited by a French connoisseur in his studio; that he was particularly mentioned in the voluminous work of the local historian during his own lifetime; that throughout his career as a painter in Delft he associated on equal terms in responsible positions with men much older than himself; that there is reason to believe that his pictures brought excellent prices during his own day because sales records show that in the years immediately following his death they sold for sums which compared favorably with those paid for the work of other men. For reasons which will be set forth later, however, Vermeer's reputation presently languished and the fame which seemed likely to be his passed him by. We see, perhaps, an early indication of this in the record of a sale of pictures less than half a century after his death when the dealer, in listing a picture by Vermeer of Delft, set forth as a selling argument that it was as good as an Eglon van der Neer.

One of the reasons why his reputation became obscured may have been because so few of his pictures came into public view. If it be true, as some scholars surmise, that his productive years, which in the nature of things could not have been much more than twenty, were really no more than ten, the number of paintings which he left behind him must still be regarded as small, even when one realizes how much time it must have taken to paint as he painted. There are not fifty well-authenticated pictures by Vermeer known to be in the world today, and the number of "lost" Vermeers, even if one includes some dubiously recorded attributions, is small. A painter whose name seldom turned up in the sales catalogues could not become widely known by that easiest of all methods of publicity—getting frequently mentioned; and with so limited a number of pictures to change hands the occasions when a Vermeer would be offered would naturally be few. And so it was perhaps not surprising, when John Smith wrote his nine-volume work on the most eminent Dutch, Flemish and French painters, in 1833, that he remarked, with curious logic, in the tiny paragraph which he devoted to Vermeer, "this painter is so little known, by reason of the scarcity of his works, that it is quite inexplicable how he attained the excellence many of them exhibit."

Inexplicable or not, "the excellence many of them exhibit" was the thing which finally brought Vermeer the fame so long denied him, for when in the middle fifties of the nineteenth century M. Thoré saw the *View of Delft* at The Hague, he was so impressed by its excellence that he set out forthwith on his quest for more pictures by its little known painter.

That was the beginning. The growth of Vermeer's fame was slow, but it was steady, and it was safe and sure. Now and then an article appeared, and now and then a book. Errors of fact and errors of surmise were repeated, after the manner of writers, from one writer to another. Slowly the obscurity was lifted, however, and the facts emerged.

Perhaps the most obvious evidence of a painter's fame is where his pictures are to be found and how much they bring in the marketplace. In Vermeer's case, of the forty-odd pictures satisfactorily ascribed to him, more than four-fifths have arrived at final and permanent homes in public museums and of the few others several are in collections which are on their way to becoming public property. The time is not far distant, therefore, when the opportunity to apply the criterion of price to a picture by Vermeer will have gone and when it will not be a matter of sensational news that an American collector has bought a Vermeer for $290,000 or that another American collector has offered his for a quarter of a million dollars. When twenty-one of Vermeer's paintings were sold in Amsterdam in 1696 they brought all told only 1404 florins, a small sum judged by modern standards, even though, as has already been said, their prices were not small by comparison with others. With scarcely more than twice as many accounted for today, Mr. James Henry Duveen has estimated the total value of the entire small number at about twenty-five million dollars (five million pounds). When the *Music Lesson* was bought as a van Mieris for King George III, it cost less than $500 (£100); now it is said to be worth from $400,000 to $500,-000 (£80,000 to £100,000). The *Milkwoman* sold for about $70 in 1696; some two centuries later it was bought for the Rijks Museum at Amsterdam for about $120,000 (£24,000).

The personality which through the years has eluded those whose attention can be caught only by the beating of the drum is revealed in the device of subject, in the arrangement of colours, in the registration of colour values and of edges; it does not appear in little graces of indication and handling. The man simply painted on, striving for and attaining the rightness of things, not cunning little affectations, taking mannerisms or engaging graces. He conceived and sought the best arrangement of line and colour that he could achieve. He must have had the thought, uttered or unexpressed, that if only he could make his painting just like what was before him it would comprise all the valid technical merits.

LIST OF ILLUSTRATIONS

LIST OF ILLUSTRATIONS

LIST OF ILLUSTRATIONS

LIST OF ILLUSTRATIONS

ACKNOWLEDGMENTS

I WISH TO EXPRESS my thanks to the many persons and institutions who have cooperated in making this book possible. I am grateful to The Metropolitan Museum of Art, New York, The Art Institute of Chicago, The National Gallery of Art, Washington, The San Diego Museum, California, The Frick Collection, New York.

I wish to express my appreciation to various publishers of fine color reproductions for permitting the use of their splendid publications for the making of our plates. These include:

DAVID ASHLEY, INC., representing Roberto Hoesch of Milan,

A. ROTHMANN, FINE ARTS INC., representing Anton Schroll of Vienna,

DR. ROBERT FREUND, of The Twin Editions,

ANTON SCHUTZ, of the New York Graphic Society,

ERICH HERRMANN, representing Braun and Co. of Paris, and The Medici Society of London.

HERMAN J. WECHSLER